Table of Contents

3

Husn Ara

Introduction to Neural Networks

History and Evolution of Neural Networks

1. Introduction

Neural networks, inspired by the human brain, have evolved significantly since their inception. From simple perceptron to deep learning architectures, they have revolutionized artificial intelligence (AI) and machine learning (ML). This section explores the key milestones in the development of neural networks.

2. Early Foundations (1940s–1950s)

- **McCulloch-Pitts Model (1943)**: Warren McCulloch and Walter Pitts proposed the first computational model of a neuron, demonstrating that neural networks could perform logical operations.
- **Hebbian Learning (1949)**: Donald Hebb introduced the concept of synaptic strength adaptation, forming the basis for modern learning algorithms.

3. The Perceptron Era (1950s–1960s)

- **Rosenblatt's Perceptron (1958)**: Frank Rosenblatt developed the perceptron, a simple neural network capable of binary classification.
- **Limitations Identified (1969)**: Marvin Minsky and Seymour Papert highlighted perceptron limitations, particularly its inability to solve non-linearly separable problems, leading to a decline in interest.

4. Revival and Backpropagation (1970s–1980s)

- **Neural Network Resurgence**: Researchers explored multilayer perceptrons (MLPs) to overcome previous limitations.
- **Backpropagation Algorithm (1986)**: David Rumelhart, Geoffrey Hinton, and Ronald Williams popularized backpropagation, enabling efficient training of deep networks.

5. Rise of Deep Learning (1990s–2000s)

- **Support Vector Machines and Kernel Methods**: Alternative ML methods gained popularity, but neural networks remained in development.
- **Computational Advancements**: Improved hardware, including GPUs, facilitated larger neural networks.
- **Convolutional Neural Networks (CNNs)**: Yann LeCun introduced LeNet (1998), demonstrating superior image recognition performance.

6. Deep Learning Revolution (2010s–Present)

- **Breakthroughs in AI**: Deep neural networks outperformed traditional algorithms in speech recognition, image classification, and natural language processing (NLP).
- **AlexNet (2012)**: Alex Krizhevsky's CNN won the ImageNet competition, sparking widespread deep learning adoption.
- **Generative Models**: Generative Adversarial Networks (GANs) and Transformer models like BERT and GPT revolutionized AI applications.

7. Future Directions

- **Quantum Neural Networks**: Exploring quantum computing for neural network optimization.
- **Explainable AI (XAI)**: Enhancing transparency and interpretability of deep learning models.
- **Neuromorphic Computing**: Developing hardware that mimics biological neural structures for energy-efficient AI.

8. Conclusion

The evolution of neural networks has driven major advancements in AI, shaping industries and everyday applications. As technology continues to progress, neural networks are expected to become even more powerful and efficient.

Biological Inspiration: The Human Brain Model

1. Introduction

Neural networks in artificial intelligence (AI) are inspired by the structure and function of the human brain. The biological neural system provides a foundation for designing artificial neural networks (ANNs) that can process information, learn, and adapt. This section explores the key aspects of the human brain that have influenced AI development.

2. Structure of the Human Brain

- **Neurons**: The brain consists of billions of neurons that transmit electrical and chemical signals.
- **Synapses**: Connections between neurons where information is processed and stored.
- **Neural Plasticity**: The ability of neurons to change connections and adapt based on experience.
- **Parallel Processing**: The brain processes multiple inputs simultaneously, enabling efficient cognition.

3. Comparison with Artificial Neural Networks

Feature	Human Brain	Artificial Neural Networks
Neurons	Biological cells	Artificial nodes
Synapses	Chemical & electrical signals	Weighted connections
Learning	Adaptive, experience-based	Backpropagation, optimization
Processing	Parallel, distributed	Layered, sequential

4. Key Biological Inspirations in AI

1. **Hebbian Learning**: "Neurons that fire together, wire together," influencing modern learning rules.
2. **Spiking Neural Networks (SNNs)**: AI models mimicking neuron firing patterns for real-time learning.
3. **Deep Learning and Neural Hierarchies**: Modeled after how sensory information is processed in the brain's visual and auditory cortices.
4. **Neuromorphic Computing**: Hardware designed to function like biological neurons for energy-efficient AI systems.

5. Future Directions

- **Brain-Computer Interfaces (BCIs)**: Merging AI with the human brain for direct interaction.
- **Bio-inspired AI Models**: Further mimicking the adaptability and efficiency of biological systems.
- **Cognitive Computing**: Developing AI that reasons and learns more like humans.

6. Conclusion

The human brain remains the ultimate model for AI development. By studying its structure and functions, researchers continue to advance artificial intelligence, making it more adaptive, efficient, and capable of complex problem-solving.

Artificial Neural Networks: Basics and Components

1. Introduction

Artificial Neural Networks (ANNs) are computational models inspired by the human brain's structure and functionality. They consist of interconnected processing units (neurons) that learn from data and are widely used in machine learning, deep learning, and artificial intelligence applications. This section explores the basics and key components of ANNs.

2. Basics of Artificial Neural Networks

ANNs are designed to recognize patterns and relationships in data. They operate through weighted connections and activation functions, adjusting their parameters through training processes such as backpropagation. The fundamental concept behind ANNs is that they can approximate complex functions by learning from examples.

3. Key Components of Artificial Neural Networks

3.1 Neurons (Artificial Nodes)

- **Definition**: The basic unit of an ANN, inspired by biological neurons.
- **Function**: Receives inputs, applies weights, processes information using an activation function, and passes the output to the next layer.
- **Mathematical Representation**: $y=f(\sum w_i x_i+b)$ where:
    - y = output
    - x_i = input features
    - w_i = weight associated with each input
    - b = bias term
    - f = activation function

3.2 Layers

ANNs consist of multiple layers, each serving a distinct purpose:

1. **Input Layer**: Takes raw data and passes it to the next layer.
2. **Hidden Layers**: Perform computations and extract patterns from the data.
3. **Output Layer**: Produces the final prediction or classification result.

3.3 Weights and Biases

- **Weights**: Determine the importance of each input.
- **Biases**: Adjust outputs independently of the inputs, improving flexibility.
- **Learning Process**: Weights and biases are adjusted during training to minimize error.

3.4 Activation Functions

Activation functions introduce non-linearity, enabling ANNs to model complex relationships. Common types include:

- **Sigmoid:** $f(x) = \frac{1}{1+e^{-x}}$ (used for probability-based outputs)
- **ReLU (Rectified Linear Unit):** $f(x) = \max(0, x)$ (efficient for deep networks)
- **Tanh:** $f(x) = \frac{e^x - e^{-x}}{e^x + e^{-x}}$ (ranges from -1 to 1)
- **Softmax:** Converts outputs into probabilities, used in classification tasks.

3.5 Learning Algorithms

The process of training an ANN involves:

1. **Forward Propagation**: Inputs pass through the network to generate outputs.
2. **Loss Function**: Measures the error between predicted and actual outputs.
3. **Backpropagation**: Calculates gradients to update weights and biases.
4. **Optimization Algorithms**: Methods like Stochastic Gradient Descent (SGD) and Adam optimize learning.

3.6 Types of Artificial Neural Networks

- **Feedforward Neural Networks (FNNs)**: Information flows in one direction; used in basic classification and regression.
- **Convolutional Neural Networks (CNNs)**: Specialized for image processing and computer vision.
- **Recurrent Neural Networks (RNNs)**: Handle sequential data with memory mechanisms.
- **Long Short-Term Memory Networks (LSTMs)**: Overcome vanishing gradient problems in RNNs.
- **Generative Adversarial Networks (GANs)**: Generate new data samples mimicking real data.

4. Conclusion

Artificial Neural Networks are powerful tools in AI, mimicking biological neurons to process and learn from data. Understanding their components and mechanisms allows for better implementation in various fields, including image recognition, natural language processing, and predictive analytics.

Real-World Applications of Neural Networks

1. Introduction

Neural networks have become a fundamental part of modern artificial intelligence (AI), powering various real-world applications across industries. Their ability to learn from data, recognize patterns, and make decisions has led to breakthroughs in numerous fields. This section explores key applications of neural networks.

2. Applications in Different Industries

2.1 Healthcare

- **Medical Diagnosis**: Neural networks assist in diagnosing diseases from medical images (e.g., X-rays, MRIs, CT scans) using Convolutional Neural Networks (CNNs).
- **Drug Discovery**: Deep learning models analyze molecular structures to predict drug effectiveness and accelerate pharmaceutical research.
- **Personalized Medicine**: AI-driven models tailor treatments based on patient data and genetic profiles.

2.2 Finance

- **Fraud Detection**: Neural networks detect fraudulent transactions by analyzing patterns and anomalies in financial data.
- **Algorithmic Trading**: AI-driven models predict stock market trends and execute high-frequency trades.
- **Credit Scoring**: Machine learning models assess creditworthiness by analyzing customer financial history.

2.3 Automotive Industry

- **Autonomous Vehicles**: Neural networks power self-driving cars by processing sensor data, recognizing objects, and making real-time driving decisions.
- **Driver Assistance Systems**: AI enhances features like lane detection, collision avoidance, and adaptive cruise control.

2.4 Retail and E-commerce

- **Recommendation Systems**: AI-driven models personalize product recommendations based on user behavior and preferences.
- **Demand Forecasting**: Neural networks analyze sales trends to optimize inventory and supply chain management.

- **Chatbots and Customer Support**: AI-powered virtual assistants provide automated customer support and enhance user experience.

2.5 Natural Language Processing (NLP)

- **Speech Recognition**: Neural networks enable voice assistants like Siri, Alexa, and Google Assistant to understand and process human speech.
- **Machine Translation**: AI models translate languages in real-time, improving cross-lingual communication.
- **Sentiment Analysis**: Businesses use NLP models to analyze customer feedback and social media sentiment.

2.6 Computer Vision

- **Facial Recognition**: AI-powered models identify individuals for security and authentication purposes.
- **Object Detection**: Neural networks detect and classify objects in images and videos for applications in surveillance and automation.
- **Medical Imaging**: AI enhances the accuracy of tumor detection and disease diagnosis in radiology.

2.7 Manufacturing and Robotics

- **Predictive Maintenance**: AI predicts equipment failures before they occur, reducing downtime and maintenance costs.
- **Quality Control**: Neural networks inspect products for defects, ensuring high manufacturing standards.
- **Industrial Automation**: AI-powered robots improve efficiency in assembly lines and warehouse operations.

3. Conclusion

Neural networks have revolutionized various industries by enhancing automation, decision-making, and predictive capabilities. As AI continues to advance, neural network applications will expand further, shaping the future of technology and innovation.

Mathematical Foundations

Linear Algebra for Neural Networks

1. Introduction

Linear algebra is a foundational mathematical framework used in neural networks and deep learning. It provides essential tools for handling multi-dimensional data, performing transformations, and optimizing models. This section explores key concepts of linear algebra relevant to neural networks.

2. Key Concepts in Linear Algebra for Neural Networks

2.1 Scalars, Vectors, Matrices, and Tensors

- **Scalars:** Single numerical values (e.g., a weight or bias in a neuron).

- **Vectors:** One-dimensional arrays representing input features or weights (e.g., $x = [x_1, x_2, ..., x_n]$).

- **Matrices:** Two-dimensional arrays used to represent multiple sets of weights or input data (e.g., W in fully connected layers).

- **Tensors:** Multi-dimensional generalizations of matrices (e.g., 3D images are represented as tensors with height, width, and depth).

2.2 Matrix Operations in Neural Networks

- **Addition and Subtraction:** Element-wise operations used in updating weights.

- **Matrix Multiplication:** Used for computing weighted sums in neural networks.

    - If A is an $m \times n$ matrix and B is an $n \times p$ matrix, then their product $C = AB$ is an $m \times p$ matrix.

- **Dot Product:** Computes the sum of element-wise products of two vectors, commonly used in neurons:

$$y = x \cdot w = \sum_{i=1}^{n} x_i w_i$$

- **Transpose:** Flips rows and columns of a matrix, useful in backpropagation and optimization.

2.3 Special Matrices in Neural Networks

- **Identity Matrix (I):** Used to maintain values in transformations.

- **Diagonal Matrices:** Used in regularization techniques like weight decay.

- **Sparse Matrices:** Efficiently represent large networks with few connections.

- **Orthogonal Matrices:** Used in optimization and initialization strategies.

3. Neural Network Computations Using Linear Algebra

3.1 Forward Propagation

Forward propagation uses matrix multiplications and activation functions to compute the output of a neural network:

$$Z = WX + B$$

$$Y = f(Z)$$

where:

- W = weight matrix

- X = input matrix

- B = bias vector

- Z = pre-activation values

- $f(Z)$ = activation function applied element-wise

3.2 Backpropagation and Gradients

Gradient descent, an optimization algorithm, relies on derivatives and matrix calculus to update weights:

$$W' = W - \alpha \frac{\partial L}{\partial W}$$

where:

- W' = updated weights
- α = learning rate
- L = loss function
- $\frac{\partial L}{\partial W}$ = gradient of loss with respect to weights

3.3 Eigenvalues and Singular Value Decomposition

- **Eigenvalues and Eigenvectors**: Help in dimensionality reduction and understanding weight distributions.
- **SVD**: Used in compressing deep learning models and reducing computational complexity.

4. Applications in Neural Networks

- **Principal Component Analysis (PCA)**: Reduces dimensionality of input data.
- **Convolutional Neural Networks (CNNs)**: Use matrix multiplications for feature extraction.
- **Recurrent Neural Networks (RNNs)**: Utilize vector and matrix operations for sequential data processing.
- **Optimization Techniques**: Adaptive learning rates like Adam and RMSprop rely on linear algebra computations.

5. Conclusion

Linear algebra provides the mathematical foundation for designing and optimizing neural networks. Understanding matrix operations, transformations, and gradients is essential for efficient neural network implementation and training.

Probability and Statistics Essentials in Neural Networks

Probability and statistics play a critical role in neural networks, from data preprocessing to model evaluation. They help in understanding uncertainty, making predictions, optimizing learning, and generalizing to new data. Below is a detailed breakdown of essential probability and statistics concepts used in neural networks, along with examples.

1. Probability in Neural Networks

Probability theory deals with uncertainty, and neural networks rely heavily on probabilistic methods to model complex patterns. Some essential probability concepts in neural networks include:

a) Random Variables and Probability Distributions

A **random variable** represents outcomes of a random process. Neural networks use probability distributions to model uncertainties in data and predictions.

- **Example:**
    - In image classification, the output layer of a neural network predicts probabilities for each class (e.g., dog, cat, car). These probabilities form a **categorical distribution**.

b) Conditional Probability and Bayes' Theorem

Conditional probability helps in updating beliefs based on new evidence. Bayes' theorem is particularly useful in probabilistic models such as **Bayesian Neural Networks**.

- **Example:**
    - In a spam classifier, the probability that an email is spam given certain words (e.g., "free" or "win") is computed using **Bayes' Theorem**.

c) Maximum Likelihood Estimation (MLE)

MLE is a method to estimate the parameters of a probability distribution by maximizing the likelihood of observed data.

- **Example:**
    - In logistic regression (often used as a neural network layer), MLE helps estimate weights that maximize the probability of correct classifications.

d) Softmax Function

Softmax is a probability distribution used in classification problems.

$$P(y_i) = \frac{e^{z_i}}{\sum_j e^{z_j}}$$

- **Example:**

    - In a neural network classifying handwritten digits (0-9), the softmax function ensures the output values sum to 1, representing class probabilities.

2. Statistics in Neural Networks

Statistics helps in analyzing data distributions, optimizing model performance, and preventing overfitting.

a) Mean, Variance, and Standard Deviation

Understanding data distribution is crucial before training a neural network.

- **Example**:
    - In image processing, the pixel intensity distribution (mean and variance) is used for **normalization**, ensuring stable learning.

b) Expectation and Variance

Expectation (**E[X]**) provides the average outcome of a random variable, while variance measures the spread.

- **Example**:
    - In stochastic gradient descent (SGD), understanding expectation and variance helps analyze convergence speed and stability.

c) Normal Distribution (Gaussian Distribution)

Many natural datasets follow a **normal distribution**, and neural networks often assume normally distributed weights and noise.

- **Example**:

    - **Weight Initialization**: Xavier (Glorot) initialization assumes weights should be drawn from a normal distribution with mean 0 and variance depending on the layer size.

d) Law of Large Numbers and Central Limit Theorem

- **Law of Large Numbers**: With more data, sample statistics (mean, variance) converge to true values.
- **Central Limit Theorem (CLT)**: The distribution of sample means approximates a normal distribution as sample size increases.

- **Example**:
    - In batch normalization, statistics computed from mini-batches approximate the true population distribution due to CLT.

e) Hypothesis Testing and p-Values

Hypothesis testing helps in model selection and feature importance analysis.
- **Example**:
  - In feature selection, a **t-test** can determine if a feature significantly contributes to model accuracy.

3. Probability and Statistics in Neural Network Training

Probability and statistics help in optimizing training and evaluating models.

a) Loss Functions and Cross-Entropy

Cross-entropy measures the difference between predicted probabilities and actual labels.

$$H(p, q) = -\sum p(x) \log q(x)$$

- Example:
  - In a neural network classifying emails as spam or not spam, cross-entropy quantifies prediction accuracy.

b) Regularization and Overfitting

- **L1/L2 Regularization**: Adds penalties to large weights to reduce overfitting.
- **Dropout**: Randomly drops neurons during training, acting as a probabilistic regularization technique.
- **Example**:
  - In image recognition, **dropout (p=0.5)** reduces dependency on specific neurons, improving generalization.

c) Bayesian Neural Networks (BNNs)
BNNs incorporate uncertainty by treating weights as probability distributions instead of fixed values.

- **Example**:
  - In medical diagnosis, BNNs provide uncertainty estimates alongside predictions, helping doctors make informed decisions.

4. Model Evaluation Using Statistics

Statistics are used to assess model performance.

a) Confusion Matrix and Metrics

A confusion matrix helps evaluate classification models using:

- Accuracy: $\frac{TP + TN}{Total}$
- Precision: $\frac{TP}{TP + FP}$ (relevant predictions)
- Recall: $\frac{TP}{TP + FN}$ (sensitivity)
- F1-score: Harmonic mean of precision and recall.
- Example:
  - In a cancer detection model, **high recall** ensures most positive cases are detected, even at the cost of some false positives.

b) ROC Curve and AUC

The **Receiver Operating Characteristic (ROC) curve** and **Area Under Curve (AUC)** measure classification performance across thresholds.

- **Example**:
  - In fraud detection, a high AUC means better discrimination between fraud and non-fraud transactions.

c) Bias-Variance Tradeoff

- **High Bias**: Model oversimplifies, leading to underfitting.
- **High Variance**: Model is too sensitive to training data, leading to overfitting.
- **Example**:
  - Decision trees have **high variance**, whereas linear regression has **high bias**. Neural networks balance this using **early stopping and dropout**.

Conclusion

Probability and statistics are fundamental in neural networks, influencing data preprocessing, training, optimization, and evaluation. By leveraging probabilistic models, statistical measures, and distributions, neural networks achieve robust and reliable performance across applications such as image recognition, natural language processing, and predictive analytics.

Activation Functions and Their Roles in Neural Networks

Activation functions play a critical role in neural networks by introducing non-linearity, enabling the network to learn and model complex patterns. They determine whether a neuron should be activated or not by applying a mathematical transformation to the input signal. Without activation functions, neural networks would behave like simple linear regression models, unable to capture complex relationships in data.

1. Importance of Activation Functions

Why Are Activation Functions Needed?

1. **Non-Linearity**: Most real-world data is non-linear, and activation functions allow neural networks to model complex relationships.
2. **Feature Extraction**: Different activation functions help extract features at different layers.
3. **Gradient-Based Optimization**: Activation functions affect how gradients flow during backpropagation, impacting learning efficiency.

4. **Controlling Neuron Output**: They ensure output values remain within a specific range, preventing unbounded growth.

2. Types of Activation Functions

Activation functions can be categorized into three types:

1. **Linear Activation Functions**
2. **Non-Linear Activation Functions**
3. **Advanced and Specialized Activation Functions**

3. Linear Activation Function

Linear Function (Identity Function)

$f(x)=axf(x) = axf(x)=ax$

- **Description**: The output is proportional to the input.
- **Problem**: If every layer applies a linear function, the entire network simplifies to a linear model, no matter how many layers are used.
- **Example**:
  - Used in **linear regression** but not in deep networks.

When to Use?
- Only in the **output layer** of regression problems.

4. Non-Linear Activation Functions

Non-linear activation functions help neural networks learn complex patterns. The most common non-linear activation functions include:

a) **Sigmoid Activation Function**

$$f(x) = \frac{1}{1 + e^{-x}}$$

- **Properties:**
  - ○ **Output range: (0,1)**
  - ○ **Converts input into probability-like values.**
  - ○ **Used in binary classification problems.**
- **Problems:**
  - ○ **Vanishing Gradient Problem: Gradients become very small for large or small inputs, slowing learning.**
  - ○ **Not Zero-Centered: Can cause inefficient gradient updates.**
- **Example:**
  - ○ **Used in binary classification tasks, like determining whether an email is spam or not.**

b) Hyperbolic Tangent (Tanh) Function

$$f(x) = \frac{e^x - e^{-x}}{e^x + e^{-x}}$$

- **Properties:**
  - ○ **Output range: (-1,1)**
  - ○ **Zero-centered, which helps in optimization.**
- **Problems:**
  - ○ **Vanishing Gradient Problem (though less severe than Sigmoid).**
- **Example:**
  - ○ **Used in recurrent neural networks (RNNs) for sequential data processing.**

c) Rectified Linear Unit (ReLU)

$$f(x) = \max(0, x)$$

- **Properties:**

- o **Output range: (0, ∞)**
- o **Computationally efficient.**
- o **Helps in reducing the vanishing gradient problem.**
- **Problems:**
  - o **Dying ReLU Problem: Neurons with negative inputs always output 0, leading to inactive neurons.**
- **Example:**
  - o **Convolutional Neural Networks (CNNs) for image classification.**

d) Leaky ReLU

$$f(x) = \begin{cases} x, & x > 0 \\ \alpha x, & x \leq 0 \end{cases}$$

- **Improves ReLU by allowing small negative values instead of zero.**
- **Helps avoid dying neurons.**
- **Example:**
  - o **Used in deep neural networks (DNNs) when ReLU causes dead neurons.**

e) Parametric ReLU (PReLU)

$$f(x) = \begin{cases} x, & x > 0 \\ \alpha x, & x \leq 0, \quad \text{where } \alpha \text{ is learned} \end{cases}$$

- **Adaptive version of Leaky ReLU where α is learned during training.**
- **Reduces the likelihood of dying neurons.**
- **Example:**
  - o **Used in deep networks where improved gradient flow is needed.**

f) Exponential Linear Unit (ELU)

$$f(x) = \begin{cases} x, & x > 0 \\ \alpha(e^x - 1), & x \leq 0 \end{cases}$$

- **Advantages:**
  - ○ Allows negative values, avoiding dying neurons.
  - ○ Smooth gradient, leading to better learning.
- **Example:**
  - ○ Used in deep CNNs for stability.

5. Specialized Activation Functions

Some activation functions are designed for specific tasks.
a) Softmax Function

$$P(y_i) = \frac{e^{z_i}}{\sum_j e^{z_j}}$$

- Converts outputs into probabilities (sum = 1).
- Used in multi-class classification problems.
- Example:
  - ○ In an image classifier (e.g., identifying cats, dogs, and birds), softmax outputs probabilities for each class.

b) Swish Function

$$f(x) = x \cdot \sigma(x)$$

- **Self-Gating:** The function decides its own activation.
- No dying neuron issue.
- Example:
  - ○ Used in Google's EfficientNet architecture.

c) GELU (Gaussian Error Linear Unit)

$$f(x) = x\Phi(x)$$

- **Smoother than ReLU.**
- **Used in transformers (e.g., GPT models).**

6. Choosing the Right Activation Function

Activation Function	Range	Pros	Cons	Best For
Sigmoid	(0,1)	Probabilistic output	Vanishing gradient	Binary classification
Tanh	(-1,1)	Zero-centered	Still vanishing gradient	RNNs
ReLU	(0,∞)	Fast, avoids vanishing gradients	Dying neurons	CNNs, DNNs
Leaky ReLU	(-∞,∞)	Prevents dying neurons	Needs tuning	DNNs
PReLU	(-∞,∞)	Learns best activation	More parameters	Deep networks
ELU	(-1,∞)	Smooth gradient, avoids dying neurons	Computationally expensive	CNNs
Softmax	(0,1)	Converts outputs into probabilities	Only for classification	Multi-class classification

Activation Function	Range	Pros	Cons	Best For
Swish	$(-\infty, \infty)$	Better than ReLU	More computations	EfficientNet
GELU	$(-\infty, \infty)$	Smooth, non-monotonic	Complex function	Transformers

7. Conclusion

Activation functions are crucial for neural networks as they introduce non-linearity, helping models learn complex patterns. The choice of activation function depends on the problem:

- ReLU is widely used in CNNs and DNNs.
- Sigmoid and Softmax are used in classification.
- Tanh works well for RNNs.
- Advanced functions like Swish and GELU improve performance in deep architectures.

Building Blocks of Neural Networks

Neurons and Layers

Neurons and Layers in Neural Networks

Neural networks are inspired by the structure of the human brain and consist of multiple **neurons** arranged in **layers**. These layers help process and learn patterns from data. Understanding neurons and layers is essential for designing effective deep learning models.

1. Neurons in a Neural Network

A **neuron** (also called a **node** or **perceptron**) is the fundamental unit of a neural network. Each neuron receives inputs, processes them, and produces an output, which is then passed to the next layer.

Structure of a Neuron

A neuron performs three main operations:

1. **Weighted Sum of Inputs**

    Each neuron takes multiple inputs and multiplies them by their respective weights, then adds a bias term:

    $$z = w_1 x_1 + w_2 x_2 + \cdots + w_n x_n + b$$

    - $x_i \rightarrow$ Inputs (features from data)

    - $w_i \rightarrow$ Weights (trainable parameters that adjust learning)

    - $b \rightarrow$ Bias (offset that allows shifting activation function)

2. **Activation   Function**
    The weighted sum is then passed through an **activation function** f(z) to introduce non-linearity:
    a=f(z)
    o   The activation function ensures the network can learn complex patterns.
3. **Output**
    o   The neuron's output is forwarded to the next layer or used as the final prediction.

Example: Computation of a Single Neuron

If we have:

- Inputs: $x_1 = 2, x_2 = 3$
- Weights: $w_1 = 0.5, w_2 = 0.7$
- Bias: $b = 1.0$

The neuron computes:

$$z = (0.5 \times 2) + (0.7 \times 3) + 1.0 = 3.6$$

If the **ReLU activation** is applied:

$$a = \max(0, 3.6) = 3.6$$

This value is passed to the next layer.

2. Layers in Neural Networks

A **layer** is a collection of neurons that process information together. Neural networks consist of multiple layers to extract complex features.

Types of Layers

1. **Input Layer**
2. **Hidden Layers**
3. **Output Layer**

a) Input Layer

- The first layer of a neural network.
- It receives raw data (features) and passes them to the next layer.
- **No computation** happens here; it only forwards the data.

Example: For an **image classification model** (e.g., digit recognition), if the image size is **28 × 28**, the input layer has **784 neurons (one for each pixel)**.

b) Hidden Layers

- Hidden layers perform computations by transforming inputs through weighted connections and activation functions.
- The number of hidden layers and neurons determines the network's ability to learn complex patterns.

Feature Extraction in Hidden Layers

Each hidden layer learns progressively more abstract features:

1. **First hidden layer**: Detects simple features (e.g., edges in an image).
2. **Intermediate layers**: Detect complex shapes and textures.
3. **Final layers**: Recognize high-level structures (e.g., faces, objects).

Deep vs. Shallow Networks

- **Shallow Networks**: Have 1-2 hidden layers, suitable for simple tasks.
- **Deep Networks**: Have many hidden layers, used for complex tasks like image recognition and NLP.

c) Output Layer

- The final layer in the network.
- Produces the **final prediction**.
- The number of neurons in this layer depends on the problem type:
  - **Regression**: 1 neuron (continuous output)
  - **Binary classification**: 1 neuron with Sigmoid activation (0 or 1)
  - **Multi-class classification**: One neuron per class with Softmax activation.

3. Types of Neural Network Architectures

Neural networks can have different types of layer arrangements based on the problem they solve.

a) Feedforward Neural Network (FNN)

- Information flows in **one direction** (from input to output).
- No loops or feedback.
- Used in tasks like **classification and regression.**

b) Convolutional Neural Network (CNN)

- Designed for **image processing.**
- Uses **convolutional layers** to detect spatial patterns in images.

c) Recurrent Neural Network (RNN)

- Designed for **sequential data** (e.g., time series, text).
- Has loops where outputs from previous steps influence future steps.

d) Transformer Networks

- Used in **NLP tasks** (e.g., GPT, BERT).
- Uses **self-attention mechanisms** to process sequences efficiently.

4. Types of Layers in Neural Networks

Neural networks use different types of layers for specialized tasks.

a) Fully Connected (Dense) Layers

- Each neuron is connected to every neuron in the next layer.
- Common in **feedforward networks.**

b) Convolutional Layers (CNNs)

- Extracts spatial features from images.
- Uses **filters** to detect patterns instead of full connections.

c) Recurrent Layers (RNNs)

- Maintains information over sequences using hidden states.

d) Normalization Layers

- **Batch Normalization**: Normalizes activations to stabilize training.
- **Layer Normalization**: Normalizes across features for better gradient flow.

5. Choosing the Right Number of Layers and Neurons

The choice of **layer depth and neuron count** depends on the complexity of the problem.

Factor	Shallow Network	Deep Network
Training Time	Fast	Slow
Feature Learning	Limited	Better
Data Requirement	Small dataset	Large dataset
Risk of Overfitting	Lower	Higher (needs regularization)

Hyperparameters to Consider

1. **Number of Layers**: More layers capture more complex features.
2. **Number of Neurons per Layer**: More neurons mean greater capacity but higher computational cost.
3. **Activation Functions**: Choose based on task (e.g., ReLU for hidden layers, Softmax for classification).

6. Summary

- **Neurons** process inputs using **weights, biases, and activation functions**.
- **Layers** organize neurons into structured processing stages.
- The **Input Layer** takes raw data.

- **Hidden Layers** transform features to learn patterns.
- The **Output Layer** produces the final result.
- The depth and type of layers determine the **network's capability**.

Deep Dive into Different Neural Network Architectures

Neural network architectures vary based on the type of data and problem they solve. Below, we will explore different architectures in depth, including their structures, use cases, advantages, and limitations.

1. Feedforward Neural Networks (FNN)

Overview

A **Feedforward Neural Network (FNN)** is the simplest form of an artificial neural network where information flows in one direction: from input to output. There are no loops or cycles.

Structure

- **Input Layer**: Receives raw data.
- **Hidden Layers**: Transform the data through weighted connections and activation functions.
- **Output Layer**: Produces the final result.

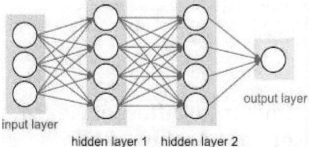

input layer

hidden layer 1   hidden layer 2

output layer

Mathematical Representation

Each neuron computes:

$$z = w_1 x_1 + w_2 x_2 + ... + w_n x_n + b$$

$$a = f(z)$$

where:

- x_i are inputs
- w_i are weights
- b is bias
- $f(z)$ is the activation function

Use Cases
- Image recognition (simple classification)
- Handwritten digit recognition (e.g., MNIST dataset)
- Stock price prediction

Advantages
- Easy to implement and train
- Suitable for structured data

Limitations
- Cannot process sequential or spatial data effectively
- Requires many parameters, leading to overfitting if not regularized

2. Convolutional Neural Networks (CNN)

Overview

A **Convolutional Neural Network (CNN)** is designed for **image and spatial data**. It extracts hierarchical patterns using convolutional layers.

Structure

1. **Convolutional Layers**: Apply filters (kernels) to extract spatial features.
2. **Pooling Layers**: Downsample feature maps to reduce dimensionality.
3. **Fully Connected Layers**: Final classification layer.

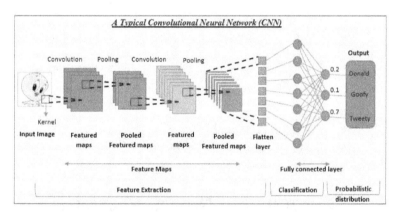

Mathematical Representation

A convolution operation:

$$h_{ij} = \sum_m \sum_n X_{i+m,j+n} W_{m,n}$$

where:

- X is the input image
- W is the filter (kernel)
- h_{ij} is the feature map

Use Cases
- Image classification (e.g., Face recognition)
- Object detection (e.g., Self-driving cars)
- Medical imaging (e.g., X-ray analysis)

Advantages
- Efficient feature extraction
- Fewer parameters compared to fully connected networks
- Translation invariance (detects objects regardless of location)

Limitations
- Requires large datasets
- Computationally expensive

3. Recurrent Neural Networks (RNN)

Overview

A **Recurrent Neural Network (RNN)** is designed for **sequential data**, where past information influences future predictions.

Structure

- **Input Layer**: Sequential inputs (e.g., words in a sentence).

44

- **Hidden Layer**: Loops to remember past information.
- **Output Layer**: Produces predictions.

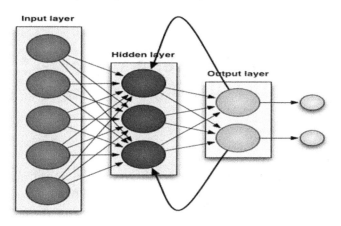

Mathematical Representation

$$h_t = f(W_h h_{t-1} + W_x x_t)$$

$$y_t = f(W_y h_t)$$

where:

- h_t is the hidden state at time t
- W_h, W_x, W_y are weight matrices
- x_t is the input at time t

Use Cases
- Text processing (e.g., Sentiment analysis, Chatbots)
- Speech recognition (e.g., Siri, Google Assistant)
- Time-series forecasting (e.g., Stock market prediction)

Advantages
- Maintains memory of past inputs
- Good for time-dependent data

Limitations

- **Vanishing Gradient Problem**: Long-term dependencies are hard to learn.
- Computationally expensive.

4. Long Short-Term Memory (LSTM)

Overview

LSTM is a special type of RNN that solves the vanishing gradient problem by using **gates** to control information flow.

Structure

1. **Forget Gate**: Decides what information to discard.
2. **Input Gate**: Decides what new information to store.
3. **Output Gate**: Produces the final output.

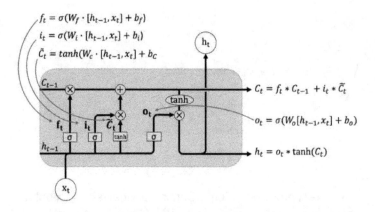

$$f_t = \sigma(W_f \cdot [h_{t-1}, x_t] + b_f)$$
$$i_t = \sigma(W_i \cdot [h_{t-1}, x_t] + b_i)$$
$$\tilde{C}_t = tanh(W_c \cdot [h_{t-1}, x_t] + b_c$$

$$C_t = f_t * C_{t-1} + i_t * \tilde{C}_t$$

$$o_t = \sigma(W_o[h_{t-1}, x_t] + b_o)$$

$$h_t = o_t * tanh(C_t)$$

Mathematical Representation

$$f_t = \sigma(W_f \cdot [h_{t-1}, x_t] + b_f)$$

$$i_t = \sigma(W_i \cdot [h_{t-1}, x_t] + b_i)$$

$$C_t = f_t \cdot C_{t-1} + i_t \cdot \tilde{C}_t$$

where:

- f_t is the forget gate
- i_t is the input gate
- C_t is the cell state

Use Cases
- Machine translation (e.g., Google Translate)
- Chatbots (e.g., OpenAI's GPT)
- Predictive text (e.g., Smartphone keyboards)

Advantages
- Remembers long-term dependencies
- Works well with sequential data

Limitations
- Slow training
- Computationally expensive

5. Gated Recurrent Unit (GRU)

Overview

GRU is a simplified version of LSTM that removes the cell state and combines gates.

Structure

- **Update Gate**: Determines what information to keep.
- **Reset Gate**: Controls how much past information is forgotten.

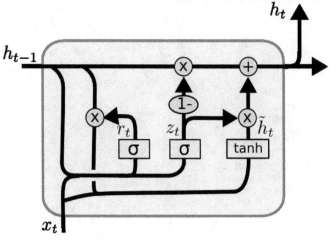

Mathematical Representation

$$z_t = \sigma(W_z \cdot [h_{t-1}, x_t])$$

$$r_t = \sigma(W_r \cdot [h_{t-1}, x_t])$$

$$h_t = (1 - z_t)h_{t-1} + z_t \bar{h}_t$$

Use Cases
- Speech recognition
- Text summarization
- Time-series forecasting

Advantages
- Fewer parameters than LSTM
- Faster training

Limitations
- May not be as powerful as LSTM for long sequences

6. Transformer Networks

Overview

Transformers are the backbone of modern **Natural Language Processing (NLP)**. They use **self-attention** to process entire sequences at once.

Structure

1. **Self-Attention Mechanism**: Learns context for each word in a sentence.
2. **Positional Encoding**: Keeps order information.
3. **Multi-Head Attention**: Captures multiple perspectives of words.

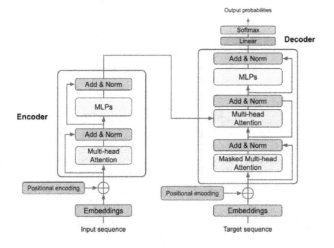

Mathematical Representation

$$\text{Attention}(Q, K, V) = \text{softmax}\left(\frac{QK^T}{\sqrt{d_k}}\right) V$$

where:

- Q, K, V are query, key, and value matrices.

Use Cases
- Machine translation (e.g., Google Translate)
- Text generation (e.g., GPT models)
- Question answering (e.g., ChatGPT)

Advantages

49

- Processes sequences **in parallel** (faster than RNNs)
- Handles **long-range dependencies** better

Limitations

- Requires huge computational power
- Needs large datasets

Comparison of Neural Network Architectures

Architecture	Best For	Key Advantage	Limitation
FNN	Structured data	Simple and easy to implement	Cannot capture spatial/sequential patterns
CNN	Image processing	Efficient feature extraction	Requires large datasets
RNN	Sequential data	Captures temporal dependencies	Suffers from vanishing gradient
LSTM	Long-term memory tasks	Handles long sequences	Computationally expensive
GRU	Sequential data	Faster than LSTM	Less powerful for very long sequences
Transformer	NLP tasks	Processes sequences in parallel	High computational cost

Conclusion

- Different neural network architectures serve different purposes.
- **FNNs** are simple and work for structured data.
- **CNNs** excel at image processing.

- **RNNs, LSTMs, and GRUs** are great for sequential data.
- **Transformers** dominate modern NLP tasks.

Supervised Learning Concepts for Neural Networks

1. Introduction

Supervised learning is a type of machine learning where a model learns from labeled data. The goal is to map inputs to correct outputs by minimizing the difference between predictions and actual labels. Neural networks excel in supervised learning tasks such as classification and regression.

2. Key Components of Supervised Learning in Neural Networks

A supervised learning model consists of:

a) Training Data
- **Input Features (XXX)**: Independent variables (e.g., pixel values in an image, words in text).
- **Output Labels (YYY)**: Known correct answers (e.g., dog or cat in an image classifier).

b) Model (Neural Network)
- **Layers**: Input, hidden, and output layers.
- **Neurons**: Process inputs using weights, biases, and activation functions.

c) Loss Function
- Measures the difference between the predicted output and actual label.

- Common loss functions:
  - **Mean Squared Error (MSE)**: Regression tasks.
  - **Binary Cross-Entropy**: Binary classification.
  - **Categorical Cross-Entropy**: Multi-class classification.

d) Optimizer
- Updates model parameters (weights and biases) to minimize the loss.
- Examples:
  - **Stochastic Gradient Descent (SGD)**
  - **Adam (Adaptive Moment Estimation)**

e) Evaluation Metrics
- Used to assess model performance.
- Examples:
  - **Accuracy, Precision, Recall, F1-score** (for classification).
  - **Mean Absolute Error (MAE), Root Mean Squared Error (RMSE)** (for regression).

3. How Supervised Learning Works in Neural Networks

Step 1: Forward Propagation

1. Input data is passed through the network.
2. Each neuron applies weights, biases, and activation functions.
3. The final layer produces predictions.

Mathematical representation:

$$z = WX + b$$

$$a = f(z)$$

Step 2: Loss Calculation

- The difference between predicted output and actual output is calculated using a **loss function**.

Step 3: Backpropagation

- **Gradient Descent** adjusts weights to minimize loss.

- Gradients ($\frac{\partial L}{\partial W}$) are computed using the **chain rule**.

Step 4: Model Update

- The optimizer updates weights:

$$W_{new} = W_{old} - \eta \frac{\partial L}{\partial W}$$

where η is the **learning rate**.

Step 5: Repeat Until Convergence
- The process continues until the loss stops decreasing.

4. Types of Supervised Learning Tasks

a) Classification
- The model predicts a **category** (e.g., cat vs. dog).
- Output layer uses **Softmax or Sigmoid activation**.

Example:
- **Email Spam Detection** (Spam or Not Spam).
- **Medical Diagnosis** (Disease Classification).

b) Regression
- The model predicts a **continuous value** (e.g., stock prices).
- Output layer is **linear (no activation function)**.

Example:
- **House Price Prediction** (Price in dollars).
- **Weather Forecasting** (Temperature in Celsius).

5. Training Process in Supervised Learning

Step	Description
1. Data Collection	Gather labeled training data.
2. Data Preprocessing	Normalize, clean, and split data.
3. Model Selection	Choose neural network architecture.
4. Training	Optimize weights using backpropagation.
5. Evaluation	Test model on unseen data.
6. Hyperparameter Tuning	Optimize learning rate, batch size, number of layers.
7. Deployment	Use model for real-world predictions.

6. Challenges in Supervised Learning for Neural Networks

a) Overfitting
- The model memorizes training data instead of generalizing.
- **Solution:** Use **dropout, L1/L2 regularization, early stopping**.

b) Underfitting
- The model is too simple and fails to learn patterns.
- **Solution:** Increase layers, train longer, use better features.

c) Data Imbalance
- Some classes appear more frequently than others.
- **Solution:** Use **class weighting, oversampling, undersampling**.

d) Computational Cost
- Large networks require significant hardware.
- **Solution:** Use **GPU acceleration, optimized architectures**.

7. Supervised Learning Example Using Neural Networks (Python)

Example: Handwritten Digit Classification (MNIST Dataset)

```
import tensorflow as tf
from tensorflow.keras.models import Sequential
from tensorflow.keras.layers import Dense, Flatten
from tensorflow.keras.optimizers import Adam
from tensorflow.keras.datasets import mnist

# Load MNIST dataset
(x_train, y_train), (x_test, y_test) = mnist.load_data()

# Normalize data
x_train, x_test = x_train / 255.0, x_test / 255.0

# Build Feedforward Neural Network
model = Sequential([
    Flatten(input_shape=(28, 28)),  # Input layer
    Dense(128, activation='relu'),  # Hidden layer
    Dense(10, activation='softmax') # Output layer (10 classes)
])

# Compile the model
model.compile(optimizer=Adam(),
        loss='sparse_categorical_crossentropy',
        metrics=['accuracy'])

# Train the model
model.fit(x_train,          y_train,          epochs=10,
validation_data=(x_test, y_test))
```

8. Conclusion

• **Supervised Learning** trains neural networks using labeled data.

• **Forward propagation, loss calculation, backpropagation, and weight updates** drive learning.

• **Classification and regression** are the two main tasks.

• **Challenges** include overfitting, underfitting, and data imbalance.

• **Real-world applications** include **image recognition, speech recognition, and finance predictions**.

Unsupervised Learning: Hebbian Theory in Neural Networks

1. Introduction to Unsupervised Learning

Unsupervised learning is a type of machine learning where a model learns patterns and relationships in data **without labeled outputs**. It is commonly used for **clustering, anomaly detection, dimensionality reduction, and feature extraction**.

Hebbian Theory
One of the most fundamental concepts in **unsupervised learning** is **Hebbian learning**, based on the biological principle that **"neurons that fire together, wire together."** Hebbian learning helps neural networks strengthen important connections based on patterns in data.

2. What is Hebbian Learning?

Hebbian learning was introduced by **Donald Hebb** in 1949 in his book *The Organization of Behavior*. The theory suggests that:

"When an axon of cell A is near enough to excite a cell B and repeatedly or persistently takes part in firing it, some growth process or metabolic change takes place in one or both cells such that A's efficiency, as one of the cells firing B, is increased."

Biological Basis
- When two neurons are **activated together**, their connection (synapse) becomes **stronger**.
- If neurons are **not activated together**, the connection **weakens**.

3. Hebbian Learning Rule

The **Hebbian learning rule** is mathematically expressed as:

$$\Delta w_{ij} = \eta \cdot x_i \cdot y_j$$

where:

- Δw_{ij} → Change in weight between neuron i and neuron j.

- η → Learning rate (controls weight adjustment speed).

- x_i → Input from neuron i.

- y_j → Output from neuron j.

Key Characteristics

☑ **Self-organizing learning**: No labeled data is required.
☑ **Positive correlation strengthening**: If two neurons activate together, the connection is strengthened.

☑ **Negative correlation weakening**: If neurons activate separately, their connection weakens.

4. Variations of Hebbian Learning

Several variations of Hebbian learning have been developed to address different learning needs:

a) Standard Hebbian Learning

$$w_{ij} = w_{ij} + \eta \cdot x_i \cdot y_j$$

- **Problem:** Weights grow indefinitely without control.

b) Normalized Hebbian Learning

$$w_{ij} = \frac{w_{ij} + \eta \cdot x_i \cdot y_j}{\sum w_{ij}^2}$$

- Prevents **unbounded weight growth** by normalizing weights.

c) Oja's Rule (Stabilized Hebbian Learning)

$$\Delta w_{ij} = \eta y_j (x_i - y_j w_{ij})$$

- Solves weight explosion by adding a **self-regulating term.**

5. Hebbian Learning in Neural Networks

Hebbian learning is primarily used for:

- **Feature learning** (extracting important patterns from data).
- **Unsupervised learning** (self-organizing networks).
- **Memory models** (associative memory, Hopfield networks).

a) Associative Memory

- **Stores patterns and recalls them when given partial input.**
- Example: Recognizing a blurry image based on past knowledge.

b) Competitive Learning Networks

- **Neurons compete** to activate based on the strength of input patterns.
- Used in **clustering algorithms** like **Self-Organizing Maps (SOMs)**.

6. Example: Hebbian Learning in Python

Simulating Hebbian Learning

```
import numpy as np

# Hebbian Learning Rule Function
def hebbian_learning(inputs):
    num_features = inputs.shape[1]
    weights = np.zeros(num_features)

    for x in inputs:
        weights += x  # Standard Hebbian Update Rule

    return weights / len(inputs)  # Normalize weights

# Example Dataset (Unlabeled)
data = np.array([
    [1, 0, 1],
    [0, 1, 1],
    [1, 1, 0],
    [0, 0, 1]
])

# Train using Hebbian Learning
weights = hebbian_learning(data)

print("Learned Weights:", weights)
```

Output:

Learned Weights: [0.5 0.5 0.75]
- The model learns **feature importance** based on input correlations.

7. Applications of Hebbian Learning

- **Self-Organizing Maps (SOMs)**: Used for clustering and visualization.
- **Principal Component Analysis (PCA)**: Reduces dimensions based on variance.
- **Hopfield Networks**: Stores and retrieves associative memory patterns.
- **Neuroscience & Cognitive Science**: Explains learning in the human brain.

8. Advantages and Limitations

Advantages	Limitations
No labeled data required	Weights can grow indefinitely
Biological plausibility	Lacks error correction like backpropagation
Good for feature extraction	Not suitable for complex deep networks

9. Conclusion

Hebbian Learning is a fundamental theory that explains **how neural connections strengthen based on co-**

activation.

- It is the foundation for **self-organizing networks, associative memory, and feature extraction**.
- Despite its simplicity, it has inspired **modern deep learning techniques** like **unsupervised representation learning**.

Training Neural Networks

Cost Functions and Optimization in Neural Networks

1. Introduction

Training a neural network involves adjusting its **weights and biases** to minimize errors and improve predictions. The key components that drive this learning process are:

- **Cost Functions**: Measure how far the network's predictions are from actual values.
- **Optimization Algorithms**: Adjust weights and biases to minimize the cost function.

Together, they help neural networks learn from data and generalize well to new inputs.

2. Cost Functions in Neural Networks

A **cost function** (also called a **loss function**) quantifies the difference between predicted and actual values. The objective is to **minimize** this error over time.

2.1 Types of Cost Functions

Cost functions are selected based on the type of machine learning task:

Task	Common Cost Function	Formula
Regression	Mean Squared Error (MSE)	$J(W) = \frac{1}{N}\sum(y_i - \hat{y}_i)^2$
Regression	Mean Absolute Error (MAE)	(J(W) = \frac{1}{N} \sum
Binary Classification	Binary Cross-Entropy (Log Loss)	$J(W) = -\frac{1}{N}\sum[y_i\log(\hat{y}_i) + (1 - y_i)\log(1 - \hat{y}_i)]$
Multi-Class Classification	Categorical Cross-Entropy	$J(W) = -\frac{1}{N}\sum\sum y_{ij}\log(\hat{y}_{ij})$

2.2 Explanation of Cost Functions

A) Mean Squared Error (MSE)

Used for **regression tasks**. It penalizes larger errors more heavily.

$$MSE = \frac{1}{N}\sum(y_i - \hat{y}_i)^2$$

- **Advantages**: Smooth and differentiable.
- **Disadvantages**: Sensitive to outliers due to squaring errors.

B) Mean Absolute Error (MAE)

Similar to MSE but takes the absolute difference.

$$MAE = \frac{1}{N}\sum|y_i - \hat{y}_i|$$

- **Advantages**: Less sensitive to outliers than MSE.
- **Disadvantages**: Not smooth (not differentiable at zero).

C) Binary Cross-Entropy

Used for **binary classification** problems. It compares the probability output to the actual label (0 or 1).

$$J(W) = -\frac{1}{N}\sum[y_i\log(\hat{y}_i) + (1 - y_i)\log(1 - \hat{y}_i)]$$

- **Advantages**: Works well for probability-based classification.
- **Disadvantages**: Requires proper probability-calibrated outputs (e.g., using a sigmoid activation).

D) Categorical Cross-Entropy

Used for **multi-class classification** with Softmax activation.

$$J(W) = -\frac{1}{N} \sum \sum y_{ij} \log(\hat{y}_{ij})$$

- **Advantages:** Works well for multi-class classification.

- **Disadvantages:** Computationally expensive for large classes.

3. Optimization in Neural Networks

Optimization is the process of minimizing the cost function by **adjusting weights and biases** using optimization algorithms.

3.1 Gradient Descent – The Core Idea

Gradient Descent is an optimization algorithm that updates parameters using the **gradient (derivative)** of the cost function.

$$W_{new} = W_{old} - \eta \frac{\partial J}{\partial W}$$

where:

- $W \rightarrow$ Weights
- $J(W) \rightarrow$ Cost function
- $\eta \rightarrow$ Learning rate (step size)

3.2 Types of Gradient Descent

Type	Description	Pros	Cons
Batch Gradient Descent (BGD)	Uses the entire dataset to compute gradients.	Stable convergence.	Slow for large datasets.
Stochastic Gradient Descent (SGD)	Updates weights after each sample.	Fast updates.	Noisy updates.
Mini-Batch Gradient Descent	Updates weights after a small batch of samples.	Balances speed and stability.	Requires tuning batch size.

3.3 Advanced Optimization Algorithms

To improve learning, advanced optimizers modify gradient descent with adaptive techniques:

A) Momentum

Momentum helps accelerate gradient descent by using past gradients.

$$V_t = \beta V_{t-1} + (1 - \beta)\frac{\partial J}{\partial W}$$

$$W_{new} = W_{old} - \eta V_t$$

- **Advantages:** Faster convergence, reduces oscillations.

- **Disadvantages:** Requires tuning the momentum factor (β).

B) RMSprop (Root Mean Square Propagation)

RMSprop adapts the learning rate for each parameter individually.

$$S_t = \beta S_{t-1} + (1 - \beta)\left(\frac{\partial J}{\partial W}\right)^2$$

$$W_{new} = W_{old} - \frac{\eta}{\sqrt{S_t} + \epsilon}\frac{\partial J}{\partial W}$$

- **Advantages:** Works well for non-stationary data.
- **Disadvantages:** Can lead to vanishing updates.

C) Adam (Adaptive Moment Estimation)

Adam combines **Momentum** and **RMSprop** for an adaptive learning rate.

$$m_t = \beta_1 m_{t-1} + (1 - \beta_1)\frac{\partial J}{\partial W}$$

$$v_t = \beta_2 v_{t-1} + (1 - \beta_2)\left(\frac{\partial J}{\partial W}\right)^2$$

$$W_{new} = W_{old} - \frac{\eta}{\sqrt{v_t} + \epsilon}m_t$$

- **Advantages:** Fast convergence, widely used in deep learning.
- **Disadvantages:** May not generalize well for all problems.

4. Choosing the Right Cost Function and Optimizer

Task	Recommended Cost Function	Recommended Optimizer
Regression	MSE / MAE	Adam / RMSprop
Binary Classification	Binary Cross-Entropy	SGD / Adam
Multi-Class Classification	Categorical Cross-Entropy	Adam
Large Datasets	MSE / Cross-Entropy	Mini-Batch SGD
Noisy Datasets	MSE / MAE	RMSprop

5. Example: Implementing Cost Functions and Optimizers in Python

Training a Neural Network using Adam Optimizer

```
import tensorflow as tf
from tensorflow.keras.models import Sequential
from tensorflow.keras.layers import Dense
from tensorflow.keras.optimizers import Adam

# Generate some example data
import numpy as np
X_train = np.random.rand(1000, 5)
y_train = (X_train[:, 0] + X_train[:, 1] > 1).astype(int)  # Simple
classification task

# Define a simple feedforward neural network
model = Sequential([
    Dense(10, activation='relu', input_shape=(5,)),
    Dense(5, activation='relu'),
    Dense(1, activation='sigmoid')  # Output layer for binary
classification
])
```

```
# Compile the model with Binary Cross-Entropy and Adam
optimizer
model.compile(optimizer=Adam(learning_rate=0.01),
        loss='binary_crossentropy',
        metrics=['accuracy'])

# Train the model
model.fit(X_train, y_train, epochs=50, batch_size=32)
```

6. Conclusion

✦ **Cost functions** measure how well a neural network predicts outputs.

✦ **Optimization algorithms** adjust weights to minimize the cost function.

✦ **Gradient descent and its variants (Adam, RMSprop, Momentum)** improve training efficiency.

✦ Choosing the **right cost function and optimizer** depends on the problem type.

Backpropagation Algorithm in Neural Networks

1. Introduction

Backpropagation (short for **backward propagation of errors**) is the fundamental algorithm used to train neural networks. It allows the network to adjust its **weights and biases** based on the **gradient of the cost function**, optimizing the model over time.

Why is Backpropagation Important?

☑ **Enables deep learning** by allowing multi-layer networks to learn.

☑ **Efficiently updates weights** to minimize prediction

Neural Networks Unlocked: From Basics to Advanced AI
errors.
☑ **Used with gradient descent** for optimization.

2. How Backpropagation Works

Backpropagation is a **supervised learning algorithm** that consists of two main phases:
1. **Forward Propagation** – Computes the predicted output.
2. **Backward Propagation** – Adjusts weights using the gradient of the loss function.

Key Steps in Backpropagation

1. **Initialize Weights and Biases** – Random small values.
2. **Forward Propagation** – Compute outputs and loss.
3. **Compute Gradients** – Differentiate the loss function w.r.t. weights.
4. **Backward Propagation** – Adjust weights using the gradient.
5. **Repeat Until Convergence** – Train for multiple iterations (epochs).

3. Forward Propagation – The First Phase

Before we update weights, we first **compute the output of the network** using the given weights.

Example: Simple 3-Layer Neural Network

Let's assume a neural network with:
- **Input Layer**: 2 neurons
- **Hidden Layer**: 2 neurons
- **Output Layer**: 1 neuron

Each neuron applies:

$$z = W \cdot X + b$$

$$a = f(z)$$

where:

- W = weights

- X = inputs

- b = bias

- $f(z)$ = activation function

Mathematical Representation

For a neuron:

$$z_1 = w_1 x_1 + w_2 x_2 + b$$

$$a_1 = f(z_1)$$

For the output:

$$z_{output} = w_3 a_1 + w_4 a_2 + b_{output}$$

The **loss function** computes the difference between the actual output y and predicted output $\hat{y}$.

4. Backpropagation – The Second Phase

4.1 Computing the Error

To update weights, we first compute the **error signal:**

$$E = \frac{1}{2}(y - \hat{y})^2$$

The goal is to **reduce this error** by adjusting the weights.

4.2 Computing the Gradients

To update weights, we use **gradient descent**. The gradients are computed using **partial derivatives** of the error with respect to each weight.

Using the **chain rule:**

$$\frac{\partial E}{\partial w} = \frac{\partial E}{\partial \hat{y}} \cdot \frac{\partial \hat{y}}{\partial z} \cdot \frac{\partial z}{\partial w}$$

For the output layer:

$$\delta_{\text{output}} = (y - \hat{y}) \cdot f'(z_{\text{output}})$$

For the hidden layer:

$$\delta_{\text{hidden}} = \delta_{\text{output}} \cdot W_{\text{hidden-output}} \cdot f'(z_{\text{hidden}})$$

4.3 Updating the Weights

Weights are updated using **gradient descent:**

$$W_{\text{new}} = W_{\text{old}} - \eta \frac{\partial E}{\partial W}$$

where:

- η = learning rate
- $\frac{\partial E}{\partial W}$ = gradient of the loss function

5. Backpropagation Algorithm – Step-by-Step

Step	Description
1. Initialize	Set random small values for weights and biases.
2. Forward Propagation	Compute outputs using activation functions.
3. Compute Error	Measure the difference between predicted and actual values.
4. Backward Propagation	Compute gradients using the chain rule.
5. Update Weights	Adjust weights using gradient descent.
6. Repeat	Iterate until convergence.

6. Example: Backpropagation in Python

Implementation Using NumPy

```
import numpy as np

# Sigmoid activation function and its derivative
def sigmoid(x):
    return 1 / (1 + np.exp(-x))

def sigmoid_derivative(x):
    return x * (1 - x)

# Initialize dataset (X: inputs, Y: outputs)
X = np.array([[0,0], [0,1], [1,0], [1,1]])
Y = np.array([[0], [1], [1], [0]])  # XOR problem

# Initialize weights randomly
np.random.seed(1)
weights_input_hidden = np.random.rand(2,2)
weights_hidden_output = np.random.rand(2,1)
bias_hidden = np.random.rand(1,2)
bias_output = np.random.rand(1,1)

# Training parameters
epochs = 10000
learning_rate = 0.5
```

```
# Training loop
for epoch in range(epochs):
    # Forward propagation
    hidden_input = np.dot(X, weights_input_hidden) +
bias_hidden
    hidden_output = sigmoid(hidden_input)

    final_input = np.dot(hidden_output,
weights_hidden_output) + bias_output
    final_output = sigmoid(final_input)

    # Compute error
    error = Y - final_output

    # Backward propagation
    d_output = error * sigmoid_derivative(final_output)
    d_hidden = d_output.dot(weights_hidden_output.T) *
sigmoid_derivative(hidden_output)

    # Update weights and biases
    weights_hidden_output += hidden_output.T.dot(d_output) *
learning_rate
    weights_input_hidden += X.T.dot(d_hidden) * learning_rate
    bias_output += np.sum(d_output, axis=0, keepdims=True)
* learning_rate
    bias_hidden += np.sum(d_hidden, axis=0, keepdims=True)
* learning_rate

# Test the trained model
print("Final output after training:\n", final_output)
```

7. Advantages and Limitations of Backpropagation

Advantages

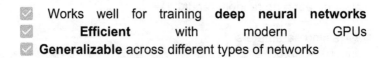

☑ Works well for training **deep neural networks**
☑ **Efficient** with modern GPUs
☑ **Generalizable** across different types of networks

Limitations

✕ **Vanishing Gradient Problem** – Small gradients slow down training in deep networks
✕ **Overfitting** – Needs regularization techniques (Dropout, L2 regularization)
✕ **Computationally Expensive** – Training deep networks requires significant resources

8. Solutions to Improve Backpropagation

- **Use ReLU Activation Function** – Helps reduce the vanishing gradient problem.
- **Batch Normalization** – Speeds up convergence.
- **Dropout Regularization** – Prevents overfitting.
- **Optimizers like Adam, RMSprop** – Improve gradient updates.

9. Summary

◆ **Backpropagation** is the backbone of deep learning, enabling neural networks to learn by adjusting weights using gradient descent.
◆ It consists of **forward propagation, error computation, gradient calculation,** and **weight updates**.
◆ **Challenges** like vanishing gradients can be addressed using **ReLU activations, batch normalization, and adaptive optimizers**.

Regularization Techniques in Neural Networks

1. Introduction

Regularization is a technique used in neural networks to prevent **overfitting**, ensuring that the model generalizes well to unseen data. Overfitting occurs when the model learns **noise** or **irrelevant details** in training data instead of true patterns.

Why is Regularization Important?

☑ **Prevents Overfitting** – Ensures the model performs well on new data.

☑ **Improves Generalization** – Reduces reliance on specific training examples.

☑ **Stabilizes Training** – Prevents extreme weight updates.

2. Types of Regularization Techniques

Several regularization techniques help improve neural network performance. The most common methods include:

Regularization Type	Purpose
L1 and L2 Regularization (Weight Decay)	Penalize large weights
Dropout	Randomly disables neurons to prevent reliance on specific features
Batch Normalization	Normalizes activations for stable learning
Early Stopping	Stops training before overfitting occurs
Data Augmentation	Generates variations of training data
Noise Injection	Adds randomness to input or hidden layers

3. L1 and L2 Regularization (Weight Decay)

Weight decay penalizes large weights by adding a **regularization term** to the loss function.

3.1 L1 Regularization (Lasso)

- Adds the **absolute value** of the weights to the loss function:

$$L = Loss + \lambda \sum |w_i|$$

- **Effect:** Encourages **sparse weights** (many weights become zero), leading to feature selection.
- **Use Case:** High-dimensional data with many irrelevant features.

3.2 L2 Regularization (Ridge)

- Adds the **square of the weights** to the loss function:

$$L = Loss + \lambda \sum w_i^2$$

- **Effect:** Reduces weight magnitude, preventing extreme values.
- **Use Case:** Stabilizes large neural networks by preventing over-reliance on any single neuron.

3.3 L1 vs. L2 Regularization

Feature	L1 (Lasso)	L2 (Ridge)
Effect on Weights	Some weights become exactly 0 (sparse model)	Weights shrink but remain nonzero
Feature Selection	Yes	No
Computational Cost	Lower	Slightly higher
Use Case	Sparse models (e.g., text data)	General deep learning

4. Dropout Regularization

Dropout is one of the most effective methods to reduce

overfitting in deep neural networks.

How Dropout Works
- **During training**: Randomly "drops" (disables) a percentage of neurons in each layer.
- **During inference**: No dropout is applied; all neurons contribute to predictions.

Mathematical Representation

For neuron h_i, dropout applies:

$$h'_i = h_i \cdot M$$

where:

- M is a **binary mask** with probability p (dropout rate).

Dropout Rate Selection

Dropout Rate	Effect
0.1 - 0.3	Recommended for small networks
0.4 - 0.6	Common for deep networks
> 0.6	May harm learning

Python Implementation

```
from tensorflow.keras.layers import Dropout

model.add(Dropout(0.5)) # 50% dropout
```

5. Batch Normalization

Batch Normalization **stabilizes training** and improves performance by normalizing activations in a layer.

How It Works

- Computes the **mean and variance** for each batch.

- Normalizes activations:

$$\hat{x} = \frac{x - \mu}{\sigma}$$

- Adds **trainable parameters** γ and β to maintain network flexibility:

$$y = \gamma\hat{x} + \beta$$

Benefits

☑ **Reduces internal covariate shift** (changes in distribution of hidden activations).
☑ **Allows higher learning rates**, speeding up training.
☑ **Acts as a regularizer**, reducing the need for dropout.

Python Implementation

from tensorflow.keras.layers import BatchNormalization

model.add(BatchNormalization())

6. Early Stopping

Early stopping prevents overfitting by **stopping training** when the validation loss **starts increasing**.

How It Works
1. Monitor the validation loss during training.
2. If loss **stops improving** for a set number of epochs; stop training.

Python Implementation

from tensorflow.keras.callbacks import EarlyStopping

early_stopping = EarlyStopping(monitor='val_loss', patience=5)
model.fit(X_train, y_train, validation_data=(X_val, y_val), callbacks=[early_stopping])

7. Data Augmentation

Data augmentation artificially **increases the training dataset size** by applying transformations such as:
- **Image rotation, flipping, cropping** (for vision tasks).
- **Synonym replacement, word shuffling** (for text tasks).
- **Adding noise, changing scale** (for numerical data).

Python Implementation (Image Augmentation)

```
from        tensorflow.keras.preprocessing.image        import
ImageDataGenerator

datagen        =        ImageDataGenerator(rotation_range=20,
horizontal_flip=True)
```

8. Noise Injection

Noise injection **forces the model to learn robust representations** by adding random noise to:

- **Input Data** (Gaussian noise in images).
- **Hidden Layers** (DropConnect: randomly disables weights).
- **Labels** (Label smoothing: prevents overconfident predictions).

Python Implementation (Gaussian Noise)

```
from tensorflow.keras.layers import GaussianNoise

model.add(GaussianNoise(0.1))  # Adds noise to inputs
```

9. Choosing the Right Regularization Method

Regularization Method	Best For
L1 Regularization	Sparse models (text, high-dimensional data)
L2 Regularization	General deep learning models
Dropout	Deep networks with large datasets
Batch Normalization	Accelerating training, deep networks
Early Stopping	When dataset is small
Data Augmentation	Computer vision, NLP tasks
Noise Injection	Improving model robustness

10. Example: Applying Regularization in a Neural Network

```
import tensorflow as tf
from tensorflow.keras.models import Sequential
from tensorflow.keras.layers import Dense, Dropout,
BatchNormalization
from tensorflow.keras.regularizers import l2

# Define model
model = Sequential([
    Dense(128, activation='relu', kernel_regularizer=l2(0.01),
input_shape=(784,)),
    BatchNormalization(),
    Dropout(0.5),
    Dense(64, activation='relu', kernel_regularizer=l2(0.01)),
    BatchNormalization(),
    Dropout(0.5),
    Dense(10, activation='softmax')    # Output layer for
classification
])

# Compile model
model.compile(optimizer='adam',
loss='categorical_crossentropy', metrics=['accuracy'])

# Train model with early stopping
```

```
early_stopping                                      =
tf.keras.callbacks.EarlyStopping(monitor='val_loss',
patience=5)
model.fit(X_train,  y_train,  validation_data=(X_val,  y_val),
epochs=50, callbacks=[early_stopping])
```

11. Summary

✓ **L1 & L2 Regularization** – Prevents large weights (L1 for sparsity, L2 for stability).
✓ **Dropout** – Disables neurons randomly to reduce reliance on specific features.
✓ **Batch Normalization** – Stabilizes learning and accelerates training.
✓ **Early Stopping** – Prevents overfitting by stopping training early.
✓ **Data Augmentation** – Expands training data using transformations.
✓ **Noise Injection** – Improves generalization by introducing randomness.

Addressing Underfitting and Overfitting in Neural Networks

1. Introduction

Neural networks are powerful models, but their effectiveness depends on how well they **fit** the data. A poorly fitted model can result in **underfitting or overfitting**:

- **Underfitting**: The model fails to learn patterns from training data.
- **Overfitting**: The model memorizes training data but fails to generalize to new data.

Both issues reduce the **accuracy and reliability** of the neural network.

2. Understanding Underfitting and Overfitting

2.1 What is Underfitting?

Underfitting occurs when the model is **too simple** to capture the complexity of the data.

Causes of Underfitting

✗ Model is **too shallow** (fewer layers or neurons).
✗ **Insufficient training** (not enough epochs).
✗ **High regularization** (weights shrink too much).
✗ **Poor feature selection** (important features missing).

How to Identify Underfitting?

✗ **Training and validation loss remain high**.
✗ **Train and test accuracy are both low**.

2.2 What is Overfitting?

Overfitting occurs when the model **memorizes the training data** instead of learning patterns that generalize to unseen data.

Causes of Overfitting

✗ **Too many parameters** (large model with many layers).
✗ **Too much training** (model memorizes noise).
✗ **Too little training data** (not enough variety).
✗ **Lack of regularization** (weights grow too large).

How to Identify Overfitting?

✗ **Training accuracy is high, but validation accuracy is low**.
✗ **Training loss decreases, but validation loss increases**.

3. Strategies to Address Underfitting

If a neural network is **underfitting**, we need to **increase its capacity** to learn patterns.

Method	How It Helps
Increase Model Complexity	Add more layers and neurons to learn better representations.
Train for More Epochs	Allows the model to learn patterns over time.
Reduce Regularization	Decrease L1/L2 regularization strength if it's restricting learning.
Improve Feature Engineering	Ensure relevant features are included.
Use a Lower Learning Rate	A higher learning rate may skip over patterns in data.

3.1 Increasing Model Complexity

- Add more **hidden layers** and **neurons**.
- Use **more advanced architectures** (CNNs, RNNs, Transformers).

Example: Increasing Complexity in TensorFlow

```
from tensorflow.keras.models import Sequential
from tensorflow.keras.layers import Dense

# Add more layers to prevent underfitting
model = Sequential([
    Dense(128, activation='relu', input_shape=(784,)),
    Dense(64, activation='relu'),
    Dense(32, activation='relu'),
    Dense(10, activation='softmax')
])
```

3.2 Training for More Epochs

82

Underfitting sometimes occurs when training stops too early.

```
model.fit(X_train,          y_train,          epochs=100,
validation_data=(X_val, y_val))
```

3.3 Reducing Regularization

L1 and L2 regularization **prevent large weights**, but excessive regularization can **suppress learning**.

```
from tensorflow.keras.regularizers import l2
```

```
# Reduce regularization strength
model.add(Dense(64,                    activation='relu',
kernel_regularizer=l2(0.0001)))
```
Solution: Lower the regularization parameter λ\lambdaλ.

4. Strategies to Address Overfitting

If a neural network is **overfitting**, we need to improve its **generalization** ability.

Method	How It Helps
Use Dropout Regularization	Randomly disables neurons to prevent over-reliance.
Early Stopping	Stops training before overfitting starts.
Batch Normalization	Stabilizes learning and reduces sensitivity to weight changes.
Increase Training Data	Helps the model learn more generalized patterns.
Use Data Augmentation	Creates variations of data (for image/text tasks).
Use Regularization (L1/L2)	Prevents excessive weight growth.

4.1 Using Dropout Regularization

Dropout **randomly removes neurons** during training, preventing co-dependency.

```
from tensorflow.keras.layers import Dropout

# Add dropout to prevent overfitting
model.add(Dropout(0.5))  # Drops 50% of neurons
```

Solution: Use **dropout rates between 0.3 and 0.5** for deep networks.

4.2 Early Stopping

Stops training **automatically** when validation loss starts increasing.

```
from tensorflow.keras.callbacks import EarlyStopping

early_stopping    =    EarlyStopping(monitor='val_loss', patience=5, restore_best_weights=True)

model.fit(X_train, y_train, validation_data=(X_val, y_val), epochs=50, callbacks=[early_stopping])
```

Solution: Monitor **validation loss** and stop training before overfitting occurs.

4.3 Batch Normalization

Batch Normalization **normalizes activations** between layers, reducing sensitivity to weight updates.

```
from tensorflow.keras.layers import BatchNormalization

model.add(BatchNormalization())
```

Solution: Use **Batch Normalization in deep networks** to prevent weight explosion.

4.4 Increasing Training Data

Overfitting happens when the model **memorizes** a small dataset.

Solution:
- ☑ Collect more real-world data
- ☑ Use data augmentation techniques

4.5 Data Augmentation (For Image Classification)

Data Augmentation **creates synthetic variations** of training images, forcing the model to generalize.

from tensorflow.keras.preprocessing.image import ImageDataGenerator

datagen = ImageDataGenerator(rotation_range=20, horizontal_flip=True)

Solution: Apply **rotation, flipping, and zooming** to expand datasets.

4.6 L1/L2 Regularization

Regularization **adds penalties** to large weights, preventing the model from relying too much on specific neurons.

from tensorflow.keras.regularizers import l1_l2

model.add(Dense(64, activation='relu', kernel_regularizer=l1_l2(l1=0.0001, l2=0.001)))

Solution: Choose **small values** for L1 and L2 to limit overfitting.

5. Comparison: Underfitting vs. Overfitting

Feature	Underfitting	Overfitting
Definition	Model is too simple	Model memorizes training data
Training Accuracy	Low	High
Validation Accuracy	Low	Decreases after some epochs
Loss Trend	High training & validation loss	Training loss ↓ but validation loss ↑

Feature	Underfitting	Overfitting
Solution	Increase model complexity, train longer	Use dropout, early stopping, data augmentation

6. Summary

✓ **Underfitting** occurs when the model is **too simple** → Solution: **Increase complexity, train longer, reduce regularization**.

✓ **Overfitting** occurs when the model **memorizes training data** → Solution: **Dropout, early stopping, batch normalization, data augmentation**.

✓ **Regularization techniques** like **L1/L2 penalties, dropout, and batch normalization** improve generalization.

✓ **More training data** always helps in reducing overfitting.

Husn Ara

Advanced Architectures

Convolutional Neural Networks (CNNs)

Convolutional Neural Networks (CNNs) are a type of deep learning model primarily used for image processing tasks like classification, object detection, and segmentation. CNNs are specifically designed to process and analyze grid-like data, such as images, by learning spatial hierarchies of features.

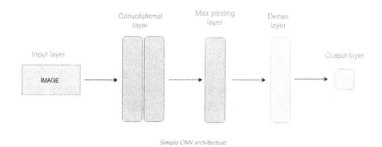

Simple CNN architecture

1. Key Components of CNNs

CNNs consist of multiple layers designed to automatically and adaptively learn spatial hierarchies of features. Below are the key components:

1.1 Convolutional Layer

The convolutional layer is the core of a CNN. It applies convolutional filters to input images to extract important features such as edges, textures, and patterns.

Mathematical Representation:

A convolution operation is defined as:

$$Y(i, j) = \sum_{m} \sum_{n} X(i + m, j + n) \cdot K(m, n)$$

where:

- X is the input image.
- K is the convolution kernel (filter).
- Y is the feature map.

1.2 Activation Function (ReLU)

After convolution, a non-linear activation function, typically **Rectified Linear Unit (ReLU)**, is applied:

f(x)=max(0,x)
ReLU helps introduce non-linearity, making the model capable of learning complex patterns.

1.3 Pooling Layer

Pooling layers reduce the spatial dimensions of feature maps while retaining the most critical information.

Types of Pooling:

- **Max Pooling**: Takes the maximum value from a region.
- **Average Pooling**: Takes the average value from a region.

Max pooling is commonly used as it preserves sharp features.

1.4 Fully Connected (FC) Layer

After multiple convolutional and pooling layers, the extracted features are flattened into a one-dimensional vector and passed through fully connected layers to make predictions.
where:

88

$$\hat{y} = W \cdot x + b$$

- W represents weights.
- b represents bias.
- x is the feature vector.

1.5 Softmax Layer (for Classification)

In multi-class classification, a **Softmax function** is applied to convert the output scores into probabilities.

$$P(y_i) = \frac{e^{y_i}}{\sum e^{y_j}}$$

2. Implementing a CNN in Python using TensorFlow/Keras

Let's implement a simple CNN model using **Keras** to classify images from the **MNIST dataset**.

```
import tensorflow as tf
from tensorflow import keras
from tensorflow.keras import layers

# Load and preprocess the MNIST dataset
(x_train,      y_train),      (x_test,      y_test)      =
keras.datasets.mnist.load_data()
x_train, x_test = x_train / 255.0, x_test / 255.0  # Normalize
pixel values

# Expand dimensions for CNN input (batch_size, height,
width, channels)
x_train = x_train.reshape(-1, 28, 28, 1)
x_test = x_test.reshape(-1, 28, 28, 1)

# Define a CNN model
model = keras.Sequential([
    layers.Conv2D(32,      (3,      3),      activation='relu',
input_shape=(28, 28, 1)),
```

```
    layers.MaxPooling2D((2, 2)),
    layers.Conv2D(64, (3, 3), activation='relu'),
    layers.MaxPooling2D((2, 2)),
    layers.Conv2D(64, (3, 3), activation='relu'),
    layers.Flatten(),
    layers.Dense(64, activation='relu'),
    layers.Dense(10, activation='softmax')  # 10 classes for
digits 0-9
])

# Compile the model
model.compile(optimizer='adam',
        loss='sparse_categorical_crossentropy',
        metrics=['accuracy'])

# Train the model
model.fit(x_train, y_train, epochs=5, validation_data=(x_test,
y_test))

# Evaluate on test data
test_loss, test_acc = model.evaluate(x_test, y_test)
print(f"Test Accuracy: {test_acc:.4f}")
```

3. Explanation of the Code

1. **Data Preparation:**
   o The MNIST dataset (handwritten digits) is loaded.
   o Normalized pixel values to range [0,1] to speed up learning.
   o Reshaped input data to match the CNN input shape (28×28×1).
2. **Building the CNN Model:**
   o **Conv2D(32, (3,3)):** First convolutional layer with 32 filters and a 3×3 kernel.
   o **MaxPooling2D((2,2)):** Reduces spatial dimensions by half.
   o **Conv2D(64, (3,3)):** Second convolutional layer with 64 filters.
   o **Flatten():** Converts the feature maps into a single vector.
   o **Dense(64, activation='relu'):** Fully connected layer.

- ○ **Dense(10, activation='softmax')**: Output layer for classification.
3. **Compiling the Model:**
  - ○ **Adam Optimizer**: An adaptive learning rate optimization technique.
  - ○ **Sparse Categorical Crossentropy Loss**: Suitable for multi-class classification.
4. **Training & Evaluating:**
  - ○ The model trains for **5 epochs**.
  - ○ It evaluates accuracy on test data.

4. CNN Applications

CNNs are widely used in:

- **Image Classification** (e.g., digit recognition, object detection).
- **Medical Imaging** (e.g., tumor detection, X-ray analysis).
- **Self-Driving Cars** (e.g., detecting pedestrians, traffic signs).
- **Facial Recognition** (e.g., unlocking phones).
- **Anomaly Detection** (e.g., detecting defective products in factories).

5. Improving CNN Performance

- **Data Augmentation**: Apply transformations (rotation, flipping) to enhance dataset diversity.
- **Dropout Layers**: Prevent overfitting by randomly dropping connections.
- **Batch Normalization**: Normalize activations to stabilize learning.
- **Transfer Learning**: Use pre-trained CNN models (e.g., VGG16, ResNet) for better accuracy.

Conclusion

Convolutional Neural Networks (CNNs) are powerful models for image recognition tasks. They efficiently capture spatial hierarchies using convolutional layers, activation functions, and pooling layers. With frameworks like TensorFlow and Keras, implementing CNNs has become straightforward.

Applications of CNNs in Computer Vision

Convolutional Neural Networks (CNNs) are widely used in various **computer vision applications**, including:

1. **Image Classification** – Identifying objects in an image (e.g., cats vs. dogs).
2. **Object Detection** – Detecting and localizing objects within an image.
3. **Image Segmentation** – Classifying each pixel in an image (e.g., medical imaging).
4. **Face Recognition** – Identifying and verifying faces in images.
5. **Handwritten Digit Recognition** – Recognizing handwritten digits (e.g., MNIST dataset).
6. **Style Transfer** – Applying artistic styles to images.
7. **Self-driving Cars** – Detecting lanes, pedestrians, and traffic signs.

1. Image Classification using CNN

We will build a **CNN-based image classifier** using the **CIFAR-10 dataset**, which contains images of 10 different objects.

Code for Image Classification using CNN

```
import tensorflow as tf
from tensorflow import keras
from tensorflow.keras import layers
import matplotlib.pyplot as plt

# Load CIFAR-10 dataset
(x_train,        y_train),        (x_test,        y_test)        =
keras.datasets.cifar10.load_data()

# Normalize pixel values (0 to 1)
x_train, x_test = x_train / 255.0, x_test / 255.0

# Define CNN model
model = keras.Sequential([
    layers.Conv2D(32,        (3,        3),        activation='relu',
input_shape=(32, 32, 3)),
    layers.MaxPooling2D((2, 2)),
    layers.Conv2D(64, (3, 3), activation='relu'),
    layers.MaxPooling2D((2, 2)),
    layers.Conv2D(128, (3, 3), activation='relu'),
    layers.MaxPooling2D((2, 2)),
    layers.Flatten(),
    layers.Dense(128, activation='relu'),
    layers.Dense(10, activation='softmax')  # 10 classes
])

# Compile the model
model.compile(optimizer='adam',
        loss='sparse_categorical_crossentropy',
        metrics=['accuracy'])

# Train the model
model.fit(x_train,              y_train,              epochs=10,
validation_data=(x_test, y_test))

# Evaluate model performance
test_loss, test_acc = model.evaluate(x_test, y_test)
print(f"Test Accuracy: {test_acc:.4f}")
```

Explanation:

- We use **CIFAR-10 dataset** (10 categories like airplanes, cars, birds, etc.).
- The CNN model consists of:
    o **Conv2D layers** for feature extraction.

- o **MaxPooling2D layers** to reduce dimensions.
- o **Flatten layer** to convert feature maps into a vector.
- o **Dense layers** to classify objects.

2. Object Detection using CNN (YOLO - Pre-trained Model)

Object detection involves **localizing multiple objects** in an image. We can use **YOLO (You Only Look Once)**, a pre-trained CNN-based model.

Code for Object Detection using YOLO

```
import cv2
import numpy as np

# Load YOLO pre-trained model
net = cv2.dnn.readNet("yolov3.weights", "yolov3.cfg")
layer_names = net.getLayerNames()
output_layers = [layer_names[i - 1] for i in
net.getUnconnectedOutLayers()]

# Load an image
image = cv2.imread("sample_image.jpg")
height, width, _ = image.shape

# Preprocess the image
blob = cv2.dnn.blobFromImage(image, 0.00392, (416, 416),
swapRB=True, crop=False)
net.setInput(blob)
outputs = net.forward(output_layers)

# Load YOLO classes
with open("coco.names", "r") as f:
    classes = [line.strip() for line in f.readlines()]

# Process YOLO outputs
boxes, confidences, class_ids = [], [], []
for output in outputs:
    for detection in output:
        scores = detection[5:]
        class_id = np.argmax(scores)
```

94

```
        confidence = scores[class_id]
        if confidence > 0.5:  # Filter detections
            center_x,   center_y,   w,   h   =   (detection[0:4]   *
width).astype("int")
            x, y = int(center_x - w / 2), int(center_y - h / 2)
            boxes.append([x, y, w, h])
            confidences.append(float(confidence))
            class_ids.append(class_id)

# Draw bounding boxes on image
for i, box in enumerate(boxes):
    x, y, w, h = box
    label = f"{classes[class_ids[i]]}: {confidences[i]:.2f}"
    cv2.rectangle(image, (x, y), (x + w, y + h), (0, 255, 0), 2)
    cv2.putText(image,     label,     (x,     y     -     10),
cv2.FONT_HERSHEY_SIMPLEX, 0.5, (0, 255, 0), 2)

# Display the image
cv2.imshow("Object Detection", image)
cv2.waitKey(0)
cv2.destroyAllWindows()
```

Explanation:

- **YOLO (You Only Look Once)** is a real-time object detection model.
- The model **identifies objects and their locations** in an image.
- We use OpenCV's **dnn module** to run YOLO on an image.

3. Image Segmentation using CNN (U-Net)

Image segmentation involves classifying **each pixel** in an image (e.g., medical tumor segmentation).

Code for Image Segmentation using U-Net

```
import tensorflow as tf
from tensorflow.keras import layers, Model

def unet_model(input_shape=(128, 128, 3)):
    inputs = layers.Input(input_shape)
```

```python
# Encoder (Downsampling)
conv1 = layers.Conv2D(64, (3, 3), activation='relu',
padding='same')(inputs)
conv1 = layers.Conv2D(64, (3, 3), activation='relu',
padding='same')(conv1)
pool1 = layers.MaxPooling2D((2, 2))(conv1)

conv2 = layers.Conv2D(128, (3, 3), activation='relu',
padding='same')(pool1)
conv2 = layers.Conv2D(128, (3, 3), activation='relu',
padding='same')(conv2)
pool2 = layers.MaxPooling2D((2, 2))(conv2)

# Decoder (Upsampling)
up1 = layers.Conv2DTranspose(64, (2, 2), strides=(2, 2),
padding='same')(pool2)
up1 = layers.concatenate([up1, conv1])
conv3 = layers.Conv2D(64, (3, 3), activation='relu',
padding='same')(up1)

outputs = layers.Conv2D(1, (1, 1),
activation='sigmoid')(conv3)

return Model(inputs, outputs)

# Create U-Net model
model = unet_model()
model.compile(optimizer='adam', loss='binary_crossentropy',
metrics=['accuracy'])
model.summary()
```

Explanation:

- **U-Net** is widely used for **medical image segmentation**.
- It consists of:
  - **Encoder** (convolutional layers) to extract features.
  - **Decoder** (upsampling layers) to reconstruct the segmented image.

Conclusion

CNNs power **many computer vision applications**:

1. **Image Classification** – Categorizing images.
2. **Object Detection** – Identifying multiple objects.
3. **Image Segmentation** – Classifying each pixel.

Using pre-trained models like **YOLO** and **U-Net**, CNNs can achieve state-of-the-art performance in various **real-world applications**.

Recurrent Neural Networks (RNNs)

1. Introduction to RNNs

Recurrent Neural Networks (RNNs) are a class of neural networks designed for **sequential data**. Unlike traditional neural networks, which process inputs independently, **RNNs have memory** and can process sequences while maintaining information about previous inputs.

Why Use RNNs?
- Suitable for tasks involving **sequential dependencies** like time series, speech recognition, and text generation.
- Maintains a **hidden state** that allows learning from past inputs.
- Unlike CNNs, which process images spatially, **RNNs process data temporally**.

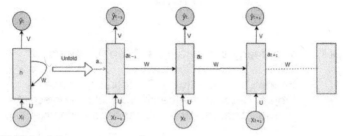

RNN Architecure

2. Structure of RNNs

An RNN processes inputs sequentially, maintaining a **hidden state** that is updated at each step.

Mathematical Representation

At each time step t:

$$h_t = f(W_x x_t + W_h h_{t-1} + b)$$

$$y_t = g(W_y h_t + c)$$

where:

- x_t = Input at time step t.
- h_t = Hidden state at t.
- y_t = Output at t.
- W_x, W_h, W_y = Weight matrices.
- b, c = Biases.
- f = Activation function (usually **tanh** or **ReLU**).
- g = Output function (e.g., **softmax** for classification).

3. Challenges of Basic RNNs

1. **Vanishing Gradient Problem** – Gradients become too small to update earlier layers effectively.
2. **Exploding Gradient Problem** – Large gradients cause instability.
3. **Short-Term Memory** – Difficulty in learning long-term dependencies.

To solve these, advanced RNN architectures like **LSTMs** and **GRUs** are used.

4. Variants of RNNs

4.1 Long Short-Term Memory (LSTM)

LSTM introduces **gates** to control information flow:
- **Forget Gate**: Decides what information to discard.
- **Input Gate**: Decides what new information to store.
- **Output Gate**: Decides what information to pass to the next time step.

4.2 Gated Recurrent Unit (GRU)
- A simplified version of LSTM with **update and reset gates**.
- **Faster training** than LSTM with similar performance.

5. Implementing RNNs in Python

Example 1: Simple RNN for Text Classification (Sentiment Analysis)

We will classify IMDB movie reviews as **positive or negative** using an RNN.

Code for Simple RNN

```
import tensorflow as tf
from tensorflow import keras
from tensorflow.keras import layers
import numpy as np
```

Neural Networks Unlocked: From Basics to Advanced AI

```
# Load IMDB dataset
max_words = 10000  # Vocabulary size
max_len = 100  # Max length of each review
(x_train,       y_train),       (x_test,       y_test)       =
keras.datasets.imdb.load_data(num_words=max_words)

# Pad sequences to ensure uniform input size
x_train                                                      =
keras.preprocessing.sequence.pad_sequences(x_train,
maxlen=max_len)
x_test                                                       =
keras.preprocessing.sequence.pad_sequences(x_test,
maxlen=max_len)

# Define an RNN model
model = keras.Sequential([
    layers.Embedding(input_dim=max_words, output_dim=32,
input_length=max_len),
    layers.SimpleRNN(32, activation='tanh'),
    layers.Dense(1, activation='sigmoid')
])

# Compile the model
model.compile(optimizer='adam',
        loss='binary_crossentropy',
        metrics=['accuracy'])

# Train the model
model.fit(x_train,    y_train,    epochs=5,    batch_size=64,
validation_data=(x_test, y_test))

# Evaluate model performance
test_loss, test_acc = model.evaluate(x_test, y_test)
print(f"Test Accuracy: {test_acc:.4f}")
```

Explanation:

1. **IMDB dataset** – Contains **movie reviews** labeled as **positive (1) or negative (0)**.
2. **Preprocessing**:
    o **Tokenization** – Converts words to numerical indices.
    o **Padding** – Ensures all inputs are of equal length.
3. **Model Architecture**:
    o **Embedding Layer** – Converts words into dense vectors.

- o **SimpleRNN Layer** – Processes sequential data.
- o **Dense Layer** – Outputs a probability for binary classification.

Example 2: LSTM for Text Classification

```
model = keras.Sequential([
    layers.Embedding(input_dim=max_words, output_dim=32,
input_length=max_len),
    layers.LSTM(64, return_sequences=False),
    layers.Dense(1, activation='sigmoid')
])

model.compile(optimizer='adam', loss='binary_crossentropy',
metrics=['accuracy'])
model.fit(x_train,    y_train,    epochs=5,    batch_size=64,
validation_data=(x_test, y_test))

test_loss, test_acc = model.evaluate(x_test, y_test)
print(f"Test Accuracy: {test_acc:.4f}")
```

Why LSTM?

- **Better memory management** with gates.
- **Handles long-term dependencies** more effectively.
- **Solves vanishing gradient problem**.

6. Applications of RNNs

RNNs are used in various **real-world applications**:

6.1 Natural Language Processing (NLP)
- **Text Classification** – Spam detection, sentiment analysis.
- **Machine Translation** – Google Translate.
- **Speech Recognition** – Siri, Google Assistant.

6.2 Time Series Prediction
- **Stock Price Forecasting** – Predicting future stock prices.
- **Weather Forecasting** – Temperature prediction.

6.3 Music and Art Generation
- **Generating music** using AI.

- **Image captioning** – Describing images in text.

7. Advanced Architectures

7.1 Bidirectional RNN (BiRNN)
- Uses both **forward and backward RNNs**.
- Useful for **text and speech processing**.

7.2 Attention Mechanism
- **Enhances focus** on important inputs.
- Used in **transformers like GPT and BERT**.

7.3 Transformer Models (GPT, BERT)
- **Replaces RNNs with self-attention**.
- Used in **ChatGPT, Google Bard**.

8. Summary

Feature	Simple RNN	LSTM	GRU
Handles long sequences	✕ (Poor)	✓ (Good)	✓ (Good)
Computational Efficiency	✓ (Fast)	✕ (Slower)	✓ (Faster)
Handles vanishing gradients	✕ (No)	✓ (Yes)	✓ (Yes)
Memory Usage	✓ (Low)	✕ (High)	✓ (Medium)

9. Conclusion

- **RNNs are powerful** for sequential tasks but suffer from **short-term memory limitations**.
- **LSTMs and GRUs** improve long-term memory and stability.

- **Transformers have replaced RNNs** in many applications (e.g., GPT, BERT).

Applications of RNNs in Natural Language Processing (NLP)

Recurrent Neural Networks (RNNs) play a significant role in **Natural Language Processing (NLP)** due to their ability to process sequential data. They help understand language structures, generate text, and model dependencies between words.

1. Key Applications of RNNs in NLP

1. **Text Classification** – Sentiment analysis, spam detection.
2. **Machine Translation** – Translating text between languages.
3. **Speech Recognition** – Converting speech to text (ASR).
4. **Chatbots & Conversational AI** – Virtual assistants like Siri, Alexa.
5. **Named Entity Recognition (NER)** – Identifying entities like names, places.
6. **Text Generation** – Generating human-like text (e.g., poetry, summaries).
7. **Speech Synthesis (Text-to-Speech, TTS)** – Converting text into speech.
8. **Grammar Checking & Auto-correction** – Spell and grammar suggestions.

2. Implementing RNN in NLP

Example 1: Sentiment Analysis using RNN
Sentiment analysis helps determine whether a given text (e.g., a movie review) has a **positive** or **negative** sentiment.

Code for Sentiment Analysis with RNN

```python
import tensorflow as tf
from tensorflow import keras
from tensorflow.keras import layers
import numpy as np

# Load IMDB dataset
max_words = 10000  # Vocabulary size
max_len = 100  # Max length of each review
(x_train,      y_train),      (x_test,      y_test)      =
keras.datasets.imdb.load_data(num_words=max_words)

# Pad sequences to ensure uniform input size
x_train                                              =
keras.preprocessing.sequence.pad_sequences(x_train,
maxlen=max_len)
x_test                                               =
keras.preprocessing.sequence.pad_sequences(x_test,
maxlen=max_len)

# Define an RNN model
model = keras.Sequential([
    layers.Embedding(input_dim=max_words, output_dim=32,
input_length=max_len),
    layers.SimpleRNN(32, activation='tanh'),
    layers.Dense(1, activation='sigmoid')
])

# Compile the model
model.compile(optimizer='adam',
        loss='binary_crossentropy',
        metrics=['accuracy'])

# Train the model
model.fit(x_train,      y_train,      epochs=5,      batch_size=64,
validation_data=(x_test, y_test))

# Evaluate model performance
```

```
test_loss, test_acc = model.evaluate(x_test, y_test)
print(f"Test Accuracy: {test_acc:.4f}")
```

Explanation

- Uses **IMDB dataset** (movie reviews labeled **positive (1)** or **negative (0)**).
- **Preprocessing**:
  - Converts words to numerical indices **(Tokenization)**.
  - Ensures all inputs are of the same length **(Padding)**.
- **Model Architecture**:
  - **Embedding Layer** – Converts words into dense vectors.
  - **SimpleRNN Layer** – Captures word dependencies.
  - **Dense Layer** – Outputs a probability for binary classification.

Example 2: Machine Translation using LSTM (English → French)

Machine translation converts text from one language to another. RNN-based **encoder-decoder** models (like seq2seq) are widely used.

```
import tensorflow as tf
from tensorflow.keras.layers import LSTM, Dense, Embedding, Input
from tensorflow.keras.models import Model
import numpy as np

# Example data (English-French)
english_sentences = ["hello", "how are you?", "I love you"]
french_sentences = ["bonjour", "comment ça va?", "je t'aime"]

# Tokenize words
tokenizer = tf.keras.preprocessing.text.Tokenizer()
tokenizer.fit_on_texts(english_sentences                    +
french_sentences)
vocab_size = len(tokenizer.word_index) + 1

# Convert text to sequences
X = tokenizer.texts_to_sequences(english_sentences)
Y = tokenizer.texts_to_sequences(french_sentences)
```

```
# Padding sequences
X   =   tf.keras.preprocessing.sequence.pad_sequences(X,
maxlen=5)
Y   =   tf.keras.preprocessing.sequence.pad_sequences(Y,
maxlen=5)

# Define LSTM-based translation model
input_layer = Input(shape=(5,))
embedding = Embedding(vocab_size, 16)(input_layer)
lstm = LSTM(64, return_sequences=True)(embedding)
output = Dense(vocab_size, activation="softmax")(lstm)

# Build model
model = Model(inputs=input_layer, outputs=output)
model.compile(loss="sparse_categorical_crossentropy",
optimizer="adam", metrics=["accuracy"])

# Train model (dummy training for demonstration)
model.fit(X, np.expand_dims(Y, -1), epochs=10)
```

Explanation
- Uses **LSTM-based Seq2Seq** (encoder-decoder model) for translation.
- **Tokenization** – Converts words into numerical sequences.
- **Embedding** – Represents words in dense vector space.
- **LSTM Layer** – Captures sequential dependencies.

Example 3: Text Generation using RNN (Character-Level)

This model generates text based on previous characters (e.g., poetry or code generation).

```
import tensorflow as tf
import numpy as np

# Sample text data
text = "hello world"
chars = sorted(set(text))  # Unique characters
char_to_index = {c: i for i, c in enumerate(chars)}
index_to_char = {i: c for i, c in enumerate(chars)}

# Convert text to sequences
seq_length = 3
X, Y = [], []
```

```
for i in range(len(text) - seq_length):
    X.append([char_to_index[c] for c in text[i:i + seq_length]])
    Y.append(char_to_index[text[i + seq_length]])

X = np.array(X)
Y = np.array(Y)

# Define RNN model
model = tf.keras.Sequential([
    tf.keras.layers.Embedding(len(chars),                16,
input_length=seq_length),
    tf.keras.layers.SimpleRNN(32, activation='relu'),
    tf.keras.layers.Dense(len(chars), activation='softmax')
])

# Compile model
model.compile(loss='sparse_categorical_crossentropy',
optimizer='adam', metrics=['accuracy'])

# Train model
model.fit(X, Y, epochs=100)

# Generate text
def generate_text(seed_text, length=5):
    for _ in range(length):
        x_input = np.array([[char_to_index[c] for c in seed_text[-
seq_length:]]])
        pred_index      =       np.argmax(model.predict(x_input,
verbose=0))
        seed_text += index_to_char[pred_index]
    return seed_text

# Test text generation
print(generate_text("hel", length=5))
```

Explanation
- Uses an **RNN to predict characters** and generate text sequences.
- Trains on **character sequences** from "hello world".
- Generates new text by predicting the next character.

3. Advanced RNN Architectures in NLP

1. **Bidirectional RNN (BiRNN)**
   - Processes text **forwards and backwards** for better understanding.
   - Used in **NER, text classification**.
2. **Attention Mechanism**
   - Enhances RNNs by **focusing on important words**.
   - Used in **Google Translate, BERT, GPT**.
3. **Transformer Models (GPT, BERT)**
   - **Replaces RNNs with self-attention**.
   - Used in **ChatGPT, Google Bard**.

4. Comparison of RNN Variants in NLP

Feature	Simple RNN	LSTM	GRU	Transformer
Handles Long Sequences	✕ (Poor)	✓ (Good)	✓ (Good)	✓ (Best)
Training Time	✓ (Fast)	✕ (Slower)	✓ (Faster)	✕ (Very Slow)
Handles Vanishing Gradients	✕ (No)	✓ (Yes)	✓ (Yes)	✓ (Yes)
Used in Modern NLP	✕ (Rare)	✓ (Yes)	✓ (Yes)	✓ (Yes)

5. Conclusion

- **RNNs are widely used** in NLP tasks like **text classification, translation, and speech recognition**.
- **LSTMs & GRUs** handle long dependencies better than simple RNNs.
- **Transformers (BERT, GPT)** have largely replaced RNNs in modern NLP.

Self-Organizing Feature Maps (SOMs) - A Detailed Explanation

1. Introduction to Self-Organizing Feature Maps (SOMs)

Self-Organizing Feature Maps (SOMs) are a type of **unsupervised artificial neural network** used for **data visualization, clustering, and dimensionality reduction**. SOMs are particularly useful for organizing and analyzing high-dimensional data in a **topology-preserving manner**.

Key Features of SOMs

☑ **Unsupervised Learning** – SOMs do not require labeled data.
☑ **Dimensionality Reduction** – Converts high-dimensional input data into a 2D representation.
☑ **Clustering** – Groups similar data points together.
☑ **Topology Preservation** – Similar data points are mapped close to each other in a 2D grid.

2. How SOMs Work

A SOM consists of a **grid of neurons** (also called nodes), where each neuron is associated with a **weight vector** of the same dimension as the input data. The learning process consists of the following steps:

Step 1: Initialize the Network
- A grid of neurons is initialized (e.g., **10×10** neurons).
- Each neuron is assigned a random weight vector with the same dimensions as the input data.

Step 2: Compute the Best Matching Unit (BMU)
- For each input sample, find the **neuron whose weight vector is closest** to the input vector.
- This neuron is called the **Best Matching Unit (BMU)** and is selected using **Euclidean distance**:

$$BMU = \arg\min_i \|X - W_i\|$$

where:

- X = input vector

- W_i = weight vector of neuron i

Step 3: Update the Weights of the BMU and its Neighbors
- The BMU and its neighboring neurons update their weight vectors to **move closer** to the input vector.
- The weight update rule is:

$$W_i(t+1) = W_i(t) + \eta(t) \cdot h(BMU, i, t) \cdot (X - W_i)$$

where:

- W_i = weight vector of neuron i

- $\eta(t)$ = learning rate (decreases over time)

- $h(BMU, i, t)$ = neighborhood function (determines how much neighbors are affected)

Step 4: Reduce Learning Rate and Neighborhood Size
- Over time, the **learning rate** and **neighborhood size** decrease, making the updates more localized.

Step 5: Repeat Until Convergence
- Steps 2-4 are repeated until the SOM stabilizes.

3. SOM Architecture

A SOM consists of:
- **Input Layer** – Each input feature is fed into the network.
- **SOM Grid (Competitive Layer)** – A **2D grid of neurons** that adjusts weights based on input patterns.

Types of SOM Grid Structures

❧ **Rectangular Grid** – Neurons are arranged in a square/rectangular   structure.
❧ **Hexagonal Grid** – Each neuron has six neighbors, allowing smoother transitions.

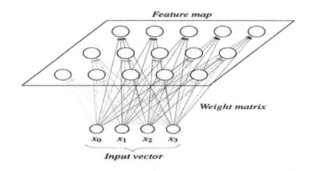

SOM Architecure

4. Applications of SOMs

SOMs are widely used in various fields for pattern recognition, clustering, and visualization:

4.1 Clustering & Data Mining
- Customer segmentation (e.g., grouping customers based on purchasing behavior).
- Market research and recommendation systems.

4.2 Image & Speech Processing

111

- Image compression and segmentation.
- Speech recognition and phoneme classification.

4.3 Anomaly Detection
- Fraud detection in banking transactions.
- Medical diagnosis (e.g., detecting tumors in MRI scans).

4.4 Dimensionality Reduction & Visualization
- High-dimensional data projection into a **2D space**.
- Used in **gene expression analysis** and **financial forecasting**.

5. Implementing SOM in Python

We will use the **MiniSom** library to implement a **Self-Organizing Map** on the **Iris dataset**.

Installation of MiniSom

pip install minisom

Code: SOM for Clustering Iris Dataset

```
import numpy as np
import matplotlib.pyplot as plt
from sklearn.datasets import load_iris
from sklearn.preprocessing import MinMaxScaler
from minisom import MiniSom

# Load the Iris dataset
iris = load_iris()
X = iris.data   # Features (sepal length, sepal width, petal length, petal width)
y = iris.target  # Labels (0, 1, 2 for three flower species)

# Normalize the data
scaler = MinMaxScaler()
X = scaler.fit_transform(X)

# Define SOM dimensions
som_x, som_y = 10, 10  # 10x10 grid
```

```
# Initialize the SOM
som = MiniSom(x=som_x, y=som_y, input_len=4, sigma=1.0,
learning_rate=0.5)

# Randomly initialize the weights
som.random_weights_init(X)

# Train the SOM (epochs = number of iterations)
som.train_random(data=X, num_iteration=1000)

# Plot the SOM output
plt.figure(figsize=(10, 10))
for i, (x, target) in enumerate(zip(X, y)):
    winner = som.winner(x)  # Get BMU coordinates
    plt.text(winner[0],  winner[1],  str(target),  color="red",
fontsize=12)

plt.xlim([0, som_x])
plt.ylim([0, som_y])
plt.title("SOM Clustering of Iris Dataset")
plt.show()
```

6. Explanation of the Code

Step 1: Load the Iris Dataset
- The dataset contains **150 samples** of **3 flower species (setosa, versicolor, virginica)**.
- Each sample has **4 features** (sepal & petal length/width).

Step 2: Data Normalization
- SOMs work better with normalized data, so we **scale values between 0 and 1**.

Step 3: Initialize and Train the SOM
- **MiniSom** is initialized with a **10×10 grid**.
- The network **trains for 1000 iterations**, updating weights dynamically.

Step 4: Visualizing the Results
- Each sample is **mapped to a neuron** in the SOM grid.

- The **species label** (0, 1, or 2) is plotted on the corresponding BMU.

7. Advantages & Limitations of SOMs

☑ **Advantages**

✔ **Unsupervised Learning** – No labeled data needed.

✔ **Powerful for High-Dimensional Data** – Reduces dimensions while preserving structure.

✔ **Intuitive Visualization** – Converts complex data into easy-to-interpret 2D maps.

✔ **Robust to Noise** – Handles noisy data well.

✖ **Limitations**

⚠ **Long Training Time** – Can take many iterations to converge.

⚠ **Fixed Grid Size** – Must predefine grid dimensions.

⚠ **Difficult to Interpret** – Results may require further clustering techniques.

8. Comparison with Other Clustering Algorithms

Feature	SOM	K-Means	PCA	t-SNE
Type	Unsupervised	Unsupervised	Dimensionality Reduction	Dimensionality Reduction
Preserves Topology?	☑ Yes	✖ No	✖ No	☑ Yes
Handles High-Dimensional Data?	☑ Yes	☑ Yes	☑ Yes	☑ Yes
Produces Clusters?	☑ Yes	☑ Yes	✖ No	✖ No

Feature	SOM	K-Means	PCA	t-SNE
Interpretability	Medium	High	High	Low
Computation Time	Medium	Fast	Fast	Slow

9. Conclusion

- **Self-Organizing Maps (SOMs)** are an excellent tool for **clustering, dimensionality reduction, and visualization**.
- They **preserve topological relationships**, making them useful in **pattern recognition, image processing, and data mining**.
- SOMs have been widely used in **market segmentation, fraud detection, and NLP**.
- Though **modern deep learning techniques** have replaced SOMs in many areas, they remain a **powerful and interpretable clustering method**.

Optical Neural Networks (ONNs): Emerging Trends

1. Introduction to Optical Neural Networks (ONNs)

Optical Neural Networks (ONNs) are a cutting-edge research area that leverages **light-based (photonic) computing** instead of traditional electronic-based neural networks. These networks use **optical components such as lasers, waveguides, and optical fibers** to perform computations, making them significantly faster and more energy-efficient than conventional deep learning models.

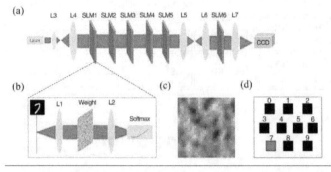

(a) & (b) Schematic of the Fourier ONN design. (c) Example of a weight mask. (d) Regions on the CCD for differentiating handwritten digits. Courtesy of AIP Advances.

Why Optical Neural Networks?

☑ **Ultra-Fast Computation** – Photons travel at the speed of light, reducing computation time.

☑ **Energy Efficiency** – Optical computing consumes much less power compared to GPUs and TPUs.

☑ **Massive Parallelism** – Multiple computations can occur simultaneously without interference.

☑ **Scalability** – Optical devices can handle large-scale neural networks efficiently.

2. How Optical Neural Networks Work

Optical Neural Networks work by **modulating and transmitting light signals** through various optical components to perform matrix multiplications, which are the core computations in deep learning.

Key Components of ONNs:

1. **Optical Linear Computation** – Performed using diffraction, interference, and optical waveguides.
2. **Nonlinear Activation Functions** – Implemented using **saturable absorbers, nonlinear crystals, or electro-optic modulators**.
3. **Optical Memory & Storage** – Optical fiber loops or quantum dots are used for data storage.

4. **Optical Interconnects** – Replace electronic connections to reduce bottlenecks in data transfer.

3. Emerging Trends in Optical Neural Networks

Recent advancements in **optical computing, nanophotonics, and quantum optics** have accelerated research in ONNs. Below are the latest **trends and breakthroughs**:

3.1 Photonic Integrated Circuits (PICs)
- Similar to **electronic chips**, but using **light-based transistors** instead of electrical transistors.
- Enables **compact, high-speed, and energy-efficient** ONNs.
- Companies like **Lightmatter and Luminous Computing** are developing PIC-based ONN hardware.

3.2 Diffractive Deep Neural Networks (D2NNs)
- Uses **light diffraction** to perform computations in free space.
- Developed by UCLA researchers, D2NNs **eliminate the need for digital processors**.
- Can be trained just like regular deep learning models using **backpropagation**.

3.3 Hybrid Optical-Electronic Networks
- Combines **optical computing for matrix multiplications** with **electronic computing for activation functions**.
- Bridges the gap between **photonic and electronic computing**.

3.4 Optical Quantum Neural Networks
- Integrates **quantum optics and neural networks** for **exponential speed-ups**.
- Uses **qubits and entanglement** to perform high-dimensional computations.

3.5 Optical Reservoir Computing

- Uses **physical optical systems** to process temporal sequences.
- Useful for **time series prediction, speech recognition, and edge computing**.

4. Applications of Optical Neural Networks

ONNs are transforming industries by enabling **high-speed, low-power AI applications**.

4.1 High-Speed Image Recognition
- ONNs can process images **thousands of times faster** than traditional CNNs.
- Used in **real-time facial recognition, medical imaging, and security systems**.

4.2 Edge AI & IoT
- Optical hardware is lightweight and can be embedded into **mobile and IoT devices**.
- Enables **low-power AI chips for wearables and smart cameras**.

4.3 Neuromorphic Computing
- ONNs mimic **biological neurons**, leading to more efficient neuromorphic chips.
- Can be used for **brain-inspired computing and autonomous systems**.

4.4 Quantum Optics & Cryptography
- Secure **optical encryption** for **high-speed, secure communication networks**.

5. Implementing Optical Neural Networks

While full ONN hardware is still in development, we can simulate optical neural networks using Python.

Example: Simulating an Optical Neural Network in Python

import numpy as np

```
import tensorflow as tf
from tensorflow.keras import layers, models

# Simulating an Optical Matrix Multiplication Layer
class OpticalLayer(layers.Layer):
    def __init__(self, units=32):
        super(OpticalLayer, self).__init__()
        self.units = units

    def build(self, input_shape):
        self.kernel = self.add_weight(shape=(input_shape[-1], self.units),
                                initializer='random_normal',
                                trainable=True)

    def call(self, inputs):
        # Simulating optical computation using matrix multiplication
        return tf.nn.relu(tf.matmul(inputs, self.kernel))

# Create a simple Optical Neural Network
model = models.Sequential([
    layers.Dense(64, activation='relu', input_shape=(100,)),  # Input layer
    OpticalLayer(32),  # Optical matrix multiplication
    layers.Dense(10, activation='softmax')  # Output layer
])

# Compile and summarize the model
model.compile(optimizer='adam',
loss='categorical_crossentropy', metrics=['accuracy'])
model.summary()
```

Explanation

- **OpticalLayer** simulates an **optical matrix multiplication unit**.
- The **model processes input data** in a way that mimics an ONN.
- Future ONN hardware can directly replace **electronic layers** with **photonic layers**.

6. Challenges & Limitations

✗ **Fabrication Complexity**

- Manufacturing **nanophotonic circuits** requires **precise engineering**.
- **High cost** of materials like **silicon photonics and metamaterials**.

✗ **Limited Nonlinear Functions**

- Optical systems are **inherently linear**, making it **difficult to implement non-linear activations**.
- Solutions include **nonlinear optical components (e.g., saturable absorbers, quantum dots)**.

✗ **Memory & Storage Constraints**

- ONNs require **optical memory** solutions for efficient data storage.
- Research is ongoing into **optical-based RAM and photonic storage devices**.

7. Future of Optical Neural Networks

Optical Neural Networks are expected to revolutionize AI and computing.

🚀 **Next-Gen AI Chips** – Companies like **Lightmatter** are building ONN-based processors.

🚀 **Quantum-Optical AI** – Hybrid **quantum photonic networks** for high-speed computing.

🚀 **Photonics in Data Centers** – Google & Microsoft exploring **optical AI accelerators** for cloud computing.

Comparison of ONNs vs Traditional AI Hardware

Feature	Optical Neural Networks	Traditional AI (GPUs/TPUs)
Computation Speed	✅ Ultra-Fast (Light-Speed)	❌ Slower (Electronic)
Energy Efficiency	✅ Low Power Consumption	❌ High Power Consumption
Parallel Processing	✅ Massive Parallelism	❌ Limited Parallelism
Scalability	✅ Highly Scalable	❌ Bottleneck at large scale
Fabrication Complexity	❌ High (Optical Components)	✅ Mature Technology

8. Conclusion

- **Optical Neural Networks (ONNs)** are **ultra-fast, energy-efficient, and scalable**.
- **Emerging trends** include **Photonic Chips, Diffractive Neural Networks, and Quantum-Optical AI**.
- **Challenges** remain in **fabrication, non-linearity, and memory storage**.
- **ONNs have the potential to replace GPUs and TPUs** for AI applications.

Practical Challenges and Solutions

Dataset Preparation and Augmentation in Neural Networks

1. Introduction to Dataset Preparation & Augmentation

For any **neural network**, the quality and quantity of the dataset significantly impact the model's performance. **Dataset preparation** ensures that data is structured, clean, and formatted correctly. **Data augmentation** artificially increases the dataset by applying transformations, improving generalization, and preventing overfitting.

2. Dataset Preparation for Neural Networks

2.1 Data Collection

Data collection is the first step and involves gathering raw data from various sources such as:
☑ **Public Datasets** – (e.g., CIFAR-10, ImageNet, MNIST, COCO, Kaggle Datasets)
☑ **Web Scraping** – Collecting text, images, or videos from online sources.

☑ **APIs & Sensors** – IoT devices, satellite data, APIs from platforms like Twitter, OpenWeather.

2.2 Data Cleaning & Preprocessing

After collecting data, it often contains missing values, noise, or irrelevant information. Preprocessing ensures the dataset is **structured and standardized** for training.

2.2.1 Handling Missing Values

☑ **Remove missing values** if their count is low.
☑ **Impute missing values** using mean, median, or deep learning   techniques.
☑ **Interpolation for time-series data** (linear, polynomial methods).

2.2.2 Data Normalization & Standardization

☑ Normalization (Min-Max Scaling):

Scales values between 0 and 1. Useful for CNNs and image data.

$$X_{normalized} = \frac{X - X_{min}}{X_{max} - X_{min}}$$

☑ Standardization (Z-score normalization):

Centers data around mean 0 with a standard deviation of 1.

$$X_{standardized} = \frac{X - \mu}{\sigma}$$

☑ Log Transformation: Useful for reducing skewness in data.

2.2.3 Data Encoding for Categorical Data

☑ **One-Hot Encoding** – Converts categorical labels into binary   vectors   (for   non-ordinal   data).
☑ **Label Encoding** – Assigns numbers to categories (for ordinal data).

2.2.4 Splitting the Dataset

The   dataset   should   be   split   into:
✓ **Training Set (70-80%)** – Used for model learning.

✓ **Validation Set (10-20%)** – Used to tune hyperparameters.
✓ **Test Set (10-15%)** – Used to evaluate model performance.

2.2.5 Data Shuffling & Batching

- **Shuffling** – Prevents learning order-dependent patterns.
- **Batching** – Divides data into batches to optimize training speed.

3. Data Augmentation

Data augmentation artificially increases the dataset size by applying **transformations**, improving generalization and robustness.

3.1 Why Data Augmentation?

✓ **Prevents Overfitting** – Reduces model dependence on specific patterns.
✓ **Improves Model Generalization** – Helps neural networks recognize variations in data.
✓ **Enhances Performance on Small Datasets** – Useful when collecting new data is expensive.

3.2 Types of Data Augmentation

3.2.1 Image Data Augmentation (Used in CNNs)

☑ **Geometric Transformations**:
- **Rotation** – Rotates image by random degrees.
- **Scaling** – Zooming in/out while maintaining aspect ratio.
- **Translation** – Shifting image along X/Y axes.
- **Flipping** – Horizontal and vertical flips.

☑ **Color Transformations**:
- **Brightness & Contrast Adjustment**
- **Color Jittering** – Alters saturation, hue, brightness randomly.

☑ **Noise Addition**:

- **Gaussian Noise** – Adds random noise to simulate real-world distortions.
- **Blur & Sharpening** – Adjusts sharpness to mimic different lighting conditions.

☑ **Cutout & Random Erasing**:
- Randomly removes parts of an image to **increase robustness**.

☑ **Mixup & CutMix**:
- **Mixup**: Blends two images and their labels.
- **CutMix**: Pastes a patch of one image into another.

Example: Image Data Augmentation in TensorFlow

```
import tensorflow as tf
from        tensorflow.keras.preprocessing.image        import
ImageDataGenerator

# Define an image data generator with augmentations
datagen = ImageDataGenerator(
    rotation_range=30,
    width_shift_range=0.2,
    height_shift_range=0.2,
    shear_range=0.2,
    zoom_range=0.2,
    horizontal_flip=True,
    fill_mode='nearest'
)

# Load an image
from tensorflow.keras.preprocessing import image
import numpy as np
import matplotlib.pyplot as plt

img = image.load_img('sample_image.jpg', target_size=(150,
150))
img_array = image.img_to_array(img)
img_array = np.expand_dims(img_array, axis=0)

# Apply data augmentation
aug_iter = datagen.flow(img_array, batch_size=1)

# Plot augmented images
plt.figure(figsize=(10,10))
for i in range(9):
```

```
    plt.subplot(3,3,i+1)
    img_aug = next(aug_iter)[0].astype('uint8')
    plt.imshow(img_aug)
    plt.axis('off')
plt.show()
```

3.2.2 Text Data Augmentation (Used in NLP)

☑ **Synonym Replacement** – Replaces words with synonyms using **WordNet**.

☑ **Back Translation** – Translates text to another language and back.

☑ **Sentence Shuffling** – Randomizes sentence order in paragraphs.

☑ **Text Insertion & Deletion** – Adds/removes random words.

Example: Text Augmentation in Python (NLTK & NLPAug)

```
import nlpaug.augmenter.word as naw

# Initialize a synonym augmentation model
synonym_aug = naw.SynonymAug(aug_src='wordnet')

sentence = "The movie was fantastic and full of surprises."
augmented_sentence = synonym_aug.augment(sentence)

print("Original:", sentence)
print("Augmented:", augmented_sentence)
```

3.2.3 Audio Data Augmentation (Used in Speech Processing)

☑ **Time Stretching** – Speeds up or slows down the audio.

☑ **Pitch Shifting** – Changes pitch without affecting speed.

☑ **Noise Injection** – Adds background noise.

Example: Audio Augmentation using Librosa

```
import librosa
import librosa.display
import numpy as np
import matplotlib.pyplot as plt

# Load an audio file
y, sr = librosa.load('audio_sample.wav')
```

```
# Apply time-stretching
y_stretch = librosa.effects.time_stretch(y, rate=1.2)

# Plot original and augmented waveforms
plt.figure(figsize=(12, 4))
librosa.display.waveshow(y,        sr=sr,        alpha=0.5,
label="Original")
librosa.display.waveshow(y_stretch,     sr=sr,     color='r',
alpha=0.5, label="Augmented")
plt.legend()
plt.show()
```

4. Dataset Preparation Best Practices

☑ **Balance the Dataset** – Ensure equal representation of all classes to prevent bias.
☑ **Use Stratified Splitting** – Maintains the proportion of labels in train-test splits.
☑ **Monitor Data Leakage** – Avoid training on test data.
☑ **Use Realistic Augmentations** – Apply only relevant transformations.

5. Conclusion

- **Dataset preparation** ensures **clean, structured, and well-formatted** data for training.
- **Data augmentation** improves generalization, enhances robustness, and prevents overfitting.
- **Different types of augmentations** exist for **images, text, and audio** data.
- **Tools like TensorFlow, NLTK, and Librosa** enable easy augmentation.

Hyperparameter Tuning in Neural Networks

1. Introduction to Hyperparameter Tuning

Hyperparameter tuning is the process of **optimizing the hyperparameters** of a neural network to achieve the **best possible performance**. Hyperparameters are settings **not learned** from the data but defined **before training** to control the learning process.

- **Why is Hyperparameter Tuning Important?**

☑ Improves model accuracy and generalization.
☑ Prevents underfitting and overfitting.
☑ Optimizes computational resources and training time.

2. Types of Hyperparameters in Neural Networks

Hyperparameters can be broadly categorized into **model, optimization, and training-related parameters**.

2.1 Model Hyperparameters

These define the architecture and structure of the neural network.

✓ **Number of Layers (Depth)** – More layers increase capacity but may lead to overfitting.
✓ **Number of Neurons (Width)** – More neurons improve representation but increase computation.
✓ **Activation Functions** – Choices include **ReLU, Sigmoid, Tanh,** **LeakyReLU**.

✓ **Dropout Rate** – Reduces overfitting by randomly dropping neurons during training.

2.2 Optimization Hyperparameters

These control the training process.
✓ **Learning Rate (α)** – Determines step size for weight updates. A **high** learning rate converges fast but may be unstable, while a **low** rate converges slowly.
✓ **Batch Size** – Number of training samples processed before updating weights.
✓ **Optimizer** – Examples include **SGD, Adam, RMSprop, Adagrad**.
✓ **Weight Initialization** – Methods include **Xavier, He, Random Normal**.

2.3 Training Hyperparameters

These determine how the model learns.
✓ **Epochs** – Number of full training passes over the dataset.
✓ **Loss Function** – Examples:

- **Binary Cross-Entropy** (for binary classification)
- **Categorical Cross-Entropy** (for multi-class classification)
- **Mean Squared Error (MSE)** (for regression tasks)

3. Methods for Hyperparameter Tuning

There are several techniques for tuning hyperparameters efficiently.

3.1 Grid Search
- Tries all possible combinations of hyperparameters.
- Computationally expensive but ensures the best setting is found.
- Used when **search space is small**.

Example: Grid Search for Learning Rate & Batch Size

```python
from sklearn.model_selection import GridSearchCV
from keras.wrappers.scikit_learn import KerasClassifier
from tensorflow.keras.models import Sequential
from tensorflow.keras.layers import Dense

# Function to create model
def create_model(learning_rate=0.01):
    model = Sequential([
        Dense(32, activation='relu', input_shape=(10,)),
        Dense(1, activation='sigmoid')
    ])

model.compile(optimizer=tf.keras.optimizers.Adam(learning_
rate=learning_rate),
            loss='binary_crossentropy', metrics=['accuracy'])
    return model

# Wrap Keras model for GridSearchCV
model = KerasClassifier(build_fn=create_model, epochs=10,
batch_size=32, verbose=0)

# Define parameter grid
param_grid = {'learning_rate': [0.001, 0.01, 0.1], 'batch_size':
[16, 32, 64]}

# Run Grid Search
grid              =              GridSearchCV(estimator=model,
param_grid=param_grid, scoring='accuracy', cv=3)
grid_result = grid.fit(X_train, y_train)

print("Best Parameters:", grid_result.best_params_)
```

☑ **Pros:** Finds the best combination exhaustively.
✗ **Cons:** Very slow for large search spaces.

3.2 Random Search
- Instead of testing all values, it **randomly selects** combinations.
- **Faster** than grid search and often finds good hyperparameters.

Example: Random Search for Learning Rate & Neurons

```python
from sklearn.model_selection import RandomizedSearchCV
```

```
import numpy as np

# Define parameter distributions
param_distributions = {'learning_rate': np.logspace(-4, -1, 10),
'neurons': [16, 32, 64, 128]}

# Run Random Search
random_search = RandomizedSearchCV(estimator=model,
param_distributions=param_distributions,          n_iter=5,
scoring='accuracy', cv=3, random_state=42)
random_result = random_search.fit(X_train, y_train)

print("Best Parameters:", random_result.best_params_)
```

✅ **Pros: Faster** than grid search while still finding good hyperparameters.

❌ **Cons:** Might miss the **optimal** combination.

3.3 Bayesian Optimization (BO)

- Instead of **random guessing**, it **models the function** using Gaussian Processes (GP).
- Finds the **best hyperparameters in fewer iterations**.

Example: Bayesian Optimization using HyperOpt

```
from hyperopt import fmin, tpe, hp, Trials

# Define the objective function
def objective(params):
    model                                         =
create_model(learning_rate=params['learning_rate'])
    history = model.fit(X_train, y_train, epochs=10, verbose=0,
validation_split=0.2)
    val_loss = min(history.history['val_loss'])
    return val_loss  # Minimize validation loss

# Define search space
space = {'learning_rate': hp.uniform('learning_rate', 0.0001,
0.1)}

# Run Bayesian Optimization
best_params       =       fmin(fn=objective,      space=space,
algo=tpe.suggest, max_evals=10)
```

```
print("Best Parameters:", best_params)
```

☑ **Pros: Efficient** for large search spaces.
✖ **Cons:** More complex than Grid/Random Search.

3.4 Hyperparameter Tuning using Optuna

Optuna is a **powerful automatic hyperparameter optimization framework**.

Example: Using Optuna to Optimize Neural Network

```
import optuna

# Define objective function
def objective(trial):
    lr = trial.suggest_loguniform('learning_rate', 0.0001, 0.1)
    neurons = trial.suggest_int('neurons', 32, 128)

    model = Sequential([
        Dense(neurons, activation='relu', input_shape=(10,)),
        Dense(1, activation='sigmoid')
    ])


model.compile(optimizer=tf.keras.optimizers.Adam(learning_
rate=lr), loss='binary_crossentropy', metrics=['accuracy'])
    history = model.fit(X_train, y_train, epochs=10, verbose=0,
validation_split=0.2)
    return min(history.history['val_loss'])  # Minimize validation
loss

# Run optimization
study = optuna.create_study(direction='minimize')
study.optimize(objective, n_trials=10)

print("Best Parameters:", study.best_params)
```

☑ **Pros: More efficient** than traditional methods.
✖ **Cons:** Requires additional setup.

4. Best Practices for Hyperparameter Tuning

- **Start with Default Values** – Use pre-tested values as a baseline.
- **Use Learning Rate Schedulers** – Adaptively reduce learning rate during training.
- **Balance Speed and Accuracy** – Avoid excessive tuning, focus on practical gains.
- **Use Transfer Learning** – Fine-tune pre-trained models instead of training from scratch.

5. Comparison of Hyperparameter Tuning Methods

Method	Pros	Cons
Grid Search	Finds best combination	Slow for large spaces
Random Search	Faster than Grid Search	May miss optimal solution
Bayesian Optimization	Efficient and adaptive	Complex setup
Optuna	State-of-the-art performance	Requires configuration

6. Conclusion

- Hyperparameter tuning **optimizes** neural networks for **better accuracy and efficiency**.
- **Grid Search** is exhaustive but slow. **Random Search** is faster but less precise.
- **Bayesian Optimization & Optuna** offer smarter, automated tuning methods.
- Choosing the right tuning method **depends on dataset size, available compute power, and model complexity**.

Transfer Learning and Pretrained Models in Neural Networks

1. Introduction to Transfer Learning

Transfer learning is a deep learning technique where a **pretrained model** (trained on a large dataset) is used as a starting point for a new task. Instead of training a neural network from scratch, we leverage the learned **features, weights, and architectures** from a model trained on a similar problem.

Why Use Transfer Learning?

☑ **Reduces Training Time** – Avoids training large models from scratch.

☑ **Requires Less Data** – Works well even with small datasets.

☑ **Improves Performance** – Uses powerful feature representations from large datasets.

☑ **Avoids Overfitting** – Generalizes better by leveraging robust pretrained features.

2. Types of Transfer Learning

2.1 Feature Extraction
- Uses pretrained model as a **feature extractor**.
- Freezes early layers and replaces the last layer for the new task.
- Example: Using **VGG16 trained on ImageNet** for medical image classification.

2.2 Fine-Tuning
- Unfreezes some layers of the pretrained model.

134

- Trains them on a new dataset **with a smaller learning rate**.
- Example: Fine-tuning **ResNet50** on satellite image classification.

3. Popular Pretrained Models for Transfer Learning

3.1 Image-Based Pretrained Models (CNNs)

Pretrained on **ImageNet** (1.2M images, 1K classes).

Model	Year	Layers	Best for
VGG16/VGG19	2014	16/19	Object classification
ResNet50/ResNet101	2015	50/101	Image recognition
InceptionV3	2016	48	Faster object detection
MobileNet	2017	28	Mobile-friendly applications
EfficientNet	2019	Varies	High accuracy with fewer parameters

3.2 NLP-Based Pretrained Models (Transformers)

Pretrained on **huge text corpora (e.g., Wikipedia, BooksCorpus)**.

Model	Year	Architecture	Use Case
BERT	2018	Transformer	Sentiment analysis, question answering
GPT-3	2020	Transformer	Text generation, chatbot
T5	2020	Encoder-Decoder	Summarization, translation
BART	2020	Transformer	Text completion, denoising

4. Transfer Learning Workflow

Step 1: Load Pretrained Model
Select a **CNN/NLP model** suitable for your task.

Step 2: Freeze Early Layers
- CNNs: Keep **lower layers** fixed (basic feature extraction).
- NLP: Keep **embedding & transformer layers** frozen.

Step 3: Modify the Last Layers
- Replace **fully connected (FC) layers** for new classification categories.
- Add a **new dense layer** with softmax activation.

Step 4: Fine-Tune the Model (Optional)
- Unfreeze **higher layers** and retrain on the new dataset.
- Use **a low learning rate (1e-4 or 1e-5)** to prevent overfitting.

5. Implementing Transfer Learning

5.1 Transfer Learning for Image Classification (Using ResNet50)

```
import tensorflow as tf
from tensorflow.keras.applications import ResNet50
from tensorflow.keras.models import Sequential
from tensorflow.keras.layers import Dense, Flatten
from        tensorflow.keras.preprocessing.image        import
ImageDataGenerator

# Load ResNet50 without the top layer
base_model      =      ResNet50(weights='imagenet',
include_top=False, input_shape=(224, 224, 3))

# Freeze the base model layers
base_model.trainable = False
```

```
# Add custom layers on top
model = Sequential([
    base_model,
    Flatten(),
    Dense(256, activation='relu'),
    Dense(3, activation='softmax')  # 3 classes
])
```

```
# Compile the model
model.compile(optimizer='adam',
loss='categorical_crossentropy', metrics=['accuracy'])
```

```
# Load dataset (example)
train_datagen = ImageDataGenerator(rescale=1./255)
train_data                                          =
train_datagen.flow_from_directory('dataset/train',
target_size=(224, 224), batch_size=32)
```

```
# Train the model
model.fit(train_data, epochs=5)
```

☑ Uses **ResNet50 pretrained on ImageNet**.
☑ **Freezes convolutional layers** & trains only the new classifier.

5.2 Fine-Tuning Pretrained Model

```
# Unfreeze the last few layers
base_model.trainable = True
for layer in base_model.layers[:-10]:  # Freeze first 90% layers
    layer.trainable = False
```

```
# Recompile with a lower learning rate
model.compile(optimizer=tf.keras.optimizers.Adam(learning_
rate=1e-4),                    loss='categorical_crossentropy',
metrics=['accuracy'])
```

```
# Train again
model.fit(train_data, epochs=5)
```

☑ **Fine-tunes the last 10 layers** to adapt to the new dataset.
☑ **Reduces the learning rate** to prevent overfitting.

5.3 Transfer Learning for NLP (Using BERT)

```
from            transformers        import            BertTokenizer,
TFBertForSequenceClassification
import tensorflow as tf

# Load Pretrained BERT Model
tokenizer      =       BertTokenizer.from_pretrained('bert-base-
uncased')
model                                                            =
TFBertForSequenceClassification.from_pretrained('bert-
base-uncased', num_labels=2)

# Tokenize input text
sentences = ["The movie was great!", "I hated the food."]
inputs       =       tokenizer(sentences,       padding=True,
truncation=True, return_tensors="tf")

# Train BERT Model
model.compile(optimizer=tf.keras.optimizers.Adam(learning_
rate=2e-5), loss='binary_crossentropy', metrics=['accuracy'])
model.fit(inputs['input_ids'], [1, 0], epochs=3)
```

☑ Uses **BERT pretrained on Wikipedia + BooksCorpus**.
☑ **Fine-tunes last layers** for binary sentiment classification.

6. When to Use Transfer Learning?

Scenario	Recommended Approach
Small dataset	Use **pretrained models** (Feature Extraction)
Large dataset	**Fine-tune** pretrained models
Domain-specific data	Use **task-specific pretrained models** (e.g., BioBERT for medical texts)
Real-time applications	Use **lightweight models** (e.g., MobileNet for mobile AI)

7. Challenges & Solutions in Transfer Learning

Challenge	Solution
Domain Mismatch (e.g., using ImageNet-trained CNN for X-ray images)	Use **domain-specific pretrained models** (e.g., CheXNet for X-rays)
Overfitting	Use **regularization** (dropout, weight decay) and **data augmentation**
Memory Issues (large pretrained models)	Use **lighter models** like MobileNet or prune unnecessary layers
Slow Training	Use **freezing layers & fine-tuning** only necessary parts

8. Transfer Learning vs. Training from Scratch

Feature	Transfer Learning	Training from Scratch
Training Time	☑ Fast (minutes to hours)	✗ Slow (days to weeks)
Data Requirement	☑ Small datasets work well	✗ Requires millions of samples
Performance	☑ High (leverages pretrained knowledge)	✗ Variable (requires lots of tuning)
Computational Cost	☑ Low (can run on a single GPU)	✗ High (requires clusters)

9. Conclusion

- **Transfer learning** is a **powerful deep learning technique** that enables AI models to perform well **even with limited data**.
- **Pretrained models** from **ImageNet, BERT, and GPT** accelerate training and improve accuracy.
- **Fine-tuning** improves **domain-specific performance** while saving computational resources.
- Future research focuses on **self-supervised learning** and **meta-learning** for even better transferability.

Husn Ara

Neural Networks in Action

Case Studies in Speech Recognition

Speech recognition has revolutionized human-computer interaction by enabling machines to **understand and process spoken language**. It is widely used in **virtual assistants, transcription services, customer support, healthcare, and accessibility tools**.

1. Introduction to Speech Recognition

Speech recognition systems use **machine learning (ML) and deep learning (DL)** to convert spoken words into text. They typically consist of:

- ☑ **Feature Extraction** (MFCC, Spectrograms)
- ☑ **Acoustic Model** (CNN, RNN, LSTM, Transformer)
- ☑ **Language Model** (N-grams, Deep Learning, GPT)

2. Case Study 1: Google Assistant – AI-Powered Speech Recognition

Background

Neural Networks Unlocked: From Basics to Advanced AI
Google Assistant is an advanced **voice-based AI assistant** used in smartphones, smart speakers, and IoT devices. It uses **deep learning-based speech recognition** to process natural conversations.

Key Technologies Used

 * **WaveNet (DeepMind)** – A generative model for text-to-speech (TTS).
 * **Transformer-based ASR models** – Uses **BERT-like models** for speech understanding.
 * **Cloud Speech-to-Text API** – Enables real-time speech recognition.

Challenges & Solutions

Challenge	Solution
Accents & Dialects	Google trained models on **global datasets** using federated learning.
Background Noise	Uses **Noise-Robust Deep Learning models**.
Real-time Processing	Deploys **edge AI models** to run directly on devices.

☑ **Impact:** Google Assistant now processes **over 1 billion voice queries per month**.

3. Case Study 2: Alexa – Improving Wake Word Detection

Background

Amazon Alexa is a **smart voice assistant** that relies on **"wake words"** (e.g., "Alexa") to activate. Ensuring **high accuracy in wake word detection** is crucial for user experience.

Key Technologies Used

 * **Deep Neural Networks (DNNs)** – Classifies wake words from background noise.

* **Recurrent Neural Networks (RNNs, LSTMs)** – Captures time-series dependencies.
* **On-Device AI Processing** – Optimized for **low-power voice processing chips**.

Challenges & Solutions

Challenge	Solution
False Positives (Detecting "Alexa" incorrectly)	Fine-tuned **LSTMs + attention mechanism**.
Multiple Speakers in a Room	Used **beamforming** with **multiple microphones**.
Latency Issues	Moved part of processing to **local devices** instead of cloud.

✅ **Impact:** Alexa's wake word accuracy improved by **30%**, reducing unintended activations.

4. Case Study 3: DeepSpeech – Open-Source Speech-to-Text by Mozilla

Background

Mozilla's **DeepSpeech** is an **open-source speech recognition system** that aims to provide high-quality, free, and privacy-preserving ASR (Automatic Speech Recognition).

Key Technologies Used

* **Deep Neural Networks (DNNs)** – Inspired by Baidu's Deep Speech model.
* **CTC (Connectionist Temporal Classification)** – Eliminates the need for word alignment.
* **Language Model (KenLM)** – Enhances word predictions.

Challenges & Solutions

Challenge	Solution
Limited Data	Crowdsourced **Common Voice Dataset** for training.
Real-Time Processing	Optimized **DeepSpeech models for edge devices**.
Multilingual Support	Built **multilingual speech models** with transfer learning.

☑ **Impact:** DeepSpeech enabled **low-cost, privacy-friendly ASR** for companies and developers.

5. Case Study 4: Medical Speech Recognition – Nuance Dragon Medical

Background

Nuance Dragon Medical is a **speech recognition software for doctors** that converts voice into structured medical notes.

Key Technologies Used

+ **Domain-Specific NLP** – Tailored for medical terminology.
+ **Acoustic Modeling** – Trained on **millions of medical voice samples**.
+ **AI-Powered Dictation** – Adapts to doctor-specific accents and speech patterns.

Challenges & Solutions

Challenge	Solution
Medical Jargon Misinterpretation	Custom **domain-adapted NLP models**.
Background Noise in Hospitals	Uses **noise-canceling AI models**.
Data Privacy Compliance	HIPAA-compliant **cloud encryption**.

☑ **Impact:** Reduced documentation time by **45%**, enabling doctors to **spend more time with patients**.

6. Case Study 5: Google Translate – Real-Time Speech Translation

Background

Google Translate introduced **real-time speech-to-text translation** to enable seamless global communication.

Key Technologies Used

* **Transformer-Based ASR** – Converts speech to text using speech **transformers**.
* **Neural Machine Translation (NMT)** – Translates text to another language.
* **TTS (Text-to-Speech)** – Reads out the translated text using **WaveNet**.

Challenges & Solutions

Challenge	Solution
Handling Different Languages	Used multilingual AI models trained on large datasets.
Grammar Errors in Translations	Added self-attention mechanism for context understanding.
Latency in Real-Time Speech Translation	Optimized speech-to-text pipeline for speed.

☑ **Impact:** Enables **instant translation** across **133+ languages**, breaking language barriers.

7. Future Trends in Speech Recognition

🚀 **Self-Supervised Learning (SSL):** AI models learning from unlabeled speech data (**Facebook's wav2vec 2.0**).
🚀 **AI-Powered Speech Synthesis:** Human-like text-to-speech synthesis (**OpenAI's Whisper**).
🚀 **Multimodal AI:** Combining speech with vision for **AI-powered assistants** (e.g., GPT-4 with voice capabilities).
🚀 **Edge AI & Low-Power ASR:** Real-time speech recognition on **IoT and mobile devices**.

8. Conclusion

- **Speech recognition is transforming industries**, from **virtual assistants (Google Assistant, Alexa)** to **medical dictation (Nuance Dragon)**.
- **Deep learning & AI advancements** have significantly improved **accuracy, real-time processing, and multilingual support**.
- The future of **AI-powered speech recognition** lies in **self-learning models, multimodal AI, and edge computing**.

Implementing Neural Networks for Industry Applications

1. Introduction

Neural networks are widely used across various industries to automate processes, improve decision-making, and enhance user experiences. Implementing a neural network for an industry application involves **data collection, model selection, training, and deployment**.

2. Industry-Specific Neural Network Applications

Industry	Application	Neural Network Used
Healthcare	Disease detection, medical imaging	CNN, RNN, Transformers
Finance	Fraud detection, stock prediction	LSTMs, GANs, Autoencoders
Retail	Customer behavior analysis, recommendation systems	CNNs, Reinforcement Learning
Manufacturing	Predictive maintenance, defect detection	CNN, RNN, Autoencoders
Automotive	Self-driving cars, traffic prediction	CNNs, RNNs, LSTMs
Agriculture	Crop monitoring, yield prediction	CNN, LSTM, Transfer Learning

3. Case Study: Implementing Neural Networks in Healthcare (Disease Detection from X-ray Images)

3.1 Problem Statement

Automate the detection of **pneumonia** from **chest X-ray images** using **Convolutional Neural Networks (CNNs)**.

3.2 Dataset

- **Dataset: Chest X-ray dataset (Kaggle)**
- **Classes:** Normal, Pneumonia

3.3 Implementation

Step 1: Install Dependencies

pip install tensorflow keras numpy matplotlib opencv-python scikit-learn

Step 2: Load Data & Preprocess

```
import tensorflow as tf
from          tensorflow.keras.preprocessing.image          import
ImageDataGenerator

# Define directories
train_dir = "dataset/train"
val_dir = "dataset/val"
test_dir = "dataset/test"

# Image Augmentation
train_datagen    =    ImageDataGenerator(rescale=1./255,
rotation_range=10, zoom_range=0.2)
val_datagen = ImageDataGenerator(rescale=1./255)

# Load data
train_data    =    train_datagen.flow_from_directory(train_dir,
target_size=(224, 224), batch_size=32, class_mode='binary')
val_data    =    val_datagen.flow_from_directory(val_dir,
target_size=(224, 224), batch_size=32, class_mode='binary')
```

Step 3: Build CNN Model

```
from tensorflow.keras.models import Sequential
from tensorflow.keras.layers import Conv2D, MaxPooling2D,
Flatten, Dense, Dropout

# CNN Architecture
model = Sequential([
    Conv2D(32, (3,3), activation='relu', input_shape=(224, 224,
3)),
    MaxPooling2D((2,2)),

    Conv2D(64, (3,3), activation='relu'),
    MaxPooling2D((2,2)),

    Flatten(),
    Dense(128, activation='relu'),
    Dropout(0.5),
```

```
    Dense(1, activation='sigmoid')  # Binary Classification
])

model.compile(optimizer='adam', loss='binary_crossentropy',
metrics=['accuracy'])
model.summary()
```

Step 4: Train Model

```
history = model.fit(train_data, validation_data=val_data,
epochs=10)
```

Step 5: Evaluate Model on Test Data

```
test_data = val_datagen.flow_from_directory(test_dir,
target_size=(224, 224), batch_size=32, class_mode='binary')
test_loss, test_acc = model.evaluate(test_data)
print(f"Test Accuracy: {test_acc:.2f}")
```

Step 6: Deploy the Model
- Convert to **TensorFlow Lite** for mobile inference.
- Deploy on **Flask API for cloud-based predictions**.

 Impact: Enables **fast, automated pneumonia detection**, assisting doctors in medical diagnosis.

4. Case Study: Implementing Neural Networks in Finance (Fraud Detection in Credit Card Transactions)

4.1 Problem Statement

Detect fraudulent credit card transactions using **Artificial Neural Networks (ANNs)**.

4.2 Dataset

- **Dataset:** Kaggle's **Credit Card Fraud Detection**
- **Classes:** Fraud (1) and Non-Fraud (0)

4.3 Implementation

Step 1: Load Data & Preprocess

```python
import pandas as pd
from sklearn.model_selection import train_test_split
from sklearn.preprocessing import StandardScaler

# Load dataset
data = pd.read_csv('creditcard.csv')

# Normalize numerical values
scaler = StandardScaler()
data['Amount'] = scaler.fit_transform(data[['Amount']])

# Split data
X = data.drop(columns=['Class'])
y = data['Class']
X_train, X_test, y_train, y_test = train_test_split(X, y,
test_size=0.2, random_state=42)
```

Step 2: Build ANN Model

```python
from tensorflow.keras.models import Sequential
from tensorflow.keras.layers import Dense

# ANN Architecture
model = Sequential([
    Dense(64,                                    activation='relu',
input_shape=(X_train.shape[1],)),
    Dense(32, activation='relu'),
    Dense(1, activation='sigmoid')  # Binary Classification
])

model.compile(optimizer='adam', loss='binary_crossentropy',
metrics=['accuracy'])
model.summary()
```

Step 3: Train Model

```python
history = model.fit(X_train, y_train, validation_data=(X_test,
y_test), epochs=10, batch_size=32)
```

Step 4: Evaluate Model

```python
loss, accuracy = model.evaluate(X_test, y_test)
print(f"Test Accuracy: {accuracy:.2f}")
```

☑ **Impact:** Helps **banks detect fraudulent transactions in real-time**, reducing financial losses.

5. Case Study: Implementing Neural Networks in Manufacturing (Defect Detection using CNNs)

5.1 Problem Statement

Automate **defect detection in products** using **computer vision and CNNs**.

5.2 Dataset

- **Dataset:** Industrial defect images
- **Classes:** Defective, Non-defective

5.3 Implementation

- **Similar to the pneumonia detection CNN** but trained on **defect images**.
- Uses **Transfer Learning (ResNet, EfficientNet)** for better accuracy.
- **Deploys model on production lines** for real-time defect analysis.

☑ **Impact:** Reduces manual inspection time, improving **quality control** in manufacturing.

6. Deployment of Neural Networks in Industry

Deployment Method	Use Case
Edge AI (Mobile, IoT)	Self-driving cars, industrial automation
Cloud-Based APIs	AI-powered financial fraud detection

Deployment Method	Use Case
Embedded AI (Healthcare Devices)	AI-assisted disease diagnosis
Web Apps (Flask/Django API)	AI chatbots, recommendation engines

7. Best Practices for Implementing Neural Networks in Industry

 Use Pretrained Models (Transfer Learning) – Reduces training time.
 Ensure Data Quality & Augmentation – Improves generalization.
 Optimize for Real-Time Inference – Use TensorFlow Lite, ONNX for mobile deployment.
 Monitor & Update Models Regularly – Continuous learning for better performance.

8. Conclusion

- **Neural networks are transforming industries** with automated AI-powered solutions.
- **CNNs, LSTMs, and Transformers** enable breakthroughs in **healthcare, finance, and manufacturing**.
- **Deployment strategies (Edge AI, Cloud APIs)** make models accessible in real-world applications.
- **Future AI systems** will focus on **faster, lightweight, and explainable AI (XAI) models**.

Neural Networks Tools and Frameworks

Neural networks are a core component of modern artificial intelligence (AI) and deep learning. To implement and train neural networks efficiently, developers rely on specialized tools and frameworks that provide optimized libraries, automatic differentiation, GPU acceleration, and pre-built models. Some of the most widely used frameworks include **TensorFlow** and **PyTorch**, along with other specialized tools.

1. TensorFlow

TensorFlow, developed by Google Brain, is an open-source deep learning framework widely used in research and production.

Features:

- **Computation Graphs:** TensorFlow uses static computation graphs, which allow for optimizations and efficient execution.
- **TensorFlow 2.0 (Eager Execution):** Supports dynamic computation graphs, making it more user-friendly.
- **GPU & TPU Support:** Built-in support for hardware acceleration.
- **TensorFlow Lite & TensorFlow.js:** Enables AI deployment on mobile devices and web applications.
- **Keras API:** TensorFlow integrates with Keras, a high-level API that simplifies model development.
- **TensorBoard:** A visualization tool for monitoring training progress.

Use Cases:

- Large-scale deep learning applications
- Production-ready AI solutions (Google, Uber, Airbnb, etc.)
- Mobile and embedded AI with TensorFlow Lite

2. PyTorch

PyTorch, developed by Facebook's AI Research lab (FAIR), is a deep learning framework known for its dynamic computation graphs and ease of use.

Features:

- **Dynamic Computation Graphs:** PyTorch uses a flexible, dynamic approach, making debugging and experimentation easier.
- **Autograd:** Automatic differentiation for gradient calculations.
- **TorchScript:** Converts models to be production-ready with optimized execution.
- **Strong Community Support:** Active development and extensive documentation.
- **Integration with NumPy:** Makes it user-friendly for researchers familiar with Python.

Use Cases:

- Academic and research-oriented deep learning
- Computer vision (integrated with OpenCV)
- Natural language processing (NLP) (used in Hugging Face models)

3. Keras

Keras is a high-level deep learning API that works as an interface for TensorFlow. It simplifies neural network design and training.

Features:

- User-friendly syntax
- Pretrained models (ResNet, VGG, MobileNet)
- Multi-backend support (TensorFlow, Theano, Microsoft CNTK)
- Suitable for beginners

Use Cases:

- Rapid prototyping
- Small-scale AI applications

4. Other Notable Frameworks

- **MXNet**: Developed by Apache, optimized for cloud-based deep learning.
- **Caffe**: Used for fast image classification tasks.
- **Theano**: One of the first deep learning frameworks, now mostly replaced by TensorFlow and PyTorch.
- **JAX**: A high-performance machine learning framework from Google, optimized for research.

Here's a comparison table summarizing the key differences between major neural network frameworks:

Feature	Tensor Flow	PyTorch	Keras	MXNet	Caffe	JAX
Developed By	Google Brain	Facebook AI	Google (Built on Tensor Flow)	Apache	UC Berkeley	Google
Computation Graph	Static (Graph-based, optimized) & Dynamic (Eager Execution)	Dynamic (Define-by-Run)	High-level API (Uses Tensor Flow backend)	Static & Dynamic	Static	Just-In-Time (JIT) Compilation
Ease of Use	Moderate	Easy (Pythonic)	Very Easy (Beginner-friendly)	Moderate	Difficult	Moderate
Performance	High (Optimi	High (Best for	Moderate	High (Opti	High (Fast	High (JIT for

155

Feature	TensorFlow	PyTorch	Keras	MXNet	Caffe	JAX
	zed for production)	research)	(Simplified, but slower)	mized for cloud)	for image tasks)	fast execution)
GPU/TPU Support	Yes (Native)	Yes (Native)	Yes (Through Tensor Flow)	Yes	Yes	Yes
Best For	Large-scale AI, Production	Research, Experimentation	Rapid Prototyping	Cloud-based AI	Image Classification	High-performance research
Pretrained Models	Yes (TensorFlow Hub)	Yes (TorchVision)	Yes	Yes (GluonCV)	Yes	No
Community Support	Large	Large	Large	Growing	Moderate	Growing
Mobile & Web Support	Yes (TensorFlow Lite, TensorFlow.js)	Limited	Yes (via Tensor Flow)	Limited	No	No
Notable Users	Google, Airbnb, Uber	Facebook, OpenAI, Tesla	Startups, Developers	Amazon, Cloud AI services	Intel, Nvidia	Google Research

Key Takeaways:

- **TensorFlow** is best for **production and deployment** (optimized for scale, supports TPUs).

- **PyTorch** is best for **research and experimentation** (flexible and Pythonic).
- **Keras** is great for **beginners and rapid prototyping**.
- **MXNet** is **optimized for cloud computing**.
- **Caffe** is used mainly for **fast image classification**.
- **JAX** is an **emerging high-performance framework** focused on **cutting-edge research**.

Conclusion

TensorFlow and PyTorch dominate the neural network landscape, with TensorFlow being production-oriented and PyTorch being research-friendly. Keras provides an easy entry point for beginners, while other frameworks like MXNet and Caffe cater to specific needs.

Future Directions

Neural Networks Beyond Deep Learning

Neural networks are commonly associated with deep learning, but they extend far beyond just deep architectures. They can be applied to various domains, including symbolic reasoning, evolutionary computation, and physics-based modeling. This discussion explores **neural networks beyond deep learning**, covering topics like spiking neural networks, neuroevolution, physics-informed neural networks, and more, with relevant code snippets.

1. Spiking Neural Networks (SNNs)

Spiking Neural Networks (SNNs) are inspired by biological neurons, where information is processed through discrete spikes rather than continuous activations.

Key Features:

- Uses event-based (spike) communication instead of real-valued signals.
- Efficient for energy-constrained environments (neuromorphic computing).
- Used in edge computing and brain-inspired AI.

Python Code: SNN with Brian2

```
from brian2 import *

# Define simulation parameters
start_scope()
```

```
tau = 10*ms
eqs = '''
dv/dt = (1-v)/tau : 1
'''

# Create a neuron group with a single neuron
G = NeuronGroup(1, eqs, threshold='v>0.8', reset='v = 0',
method='exact')
M = StateMonitor(G, 'v', record=True)

# Run the simulation
run(50*ms)

# Plot results
import matplotlib.pyplot as plt
plt.plot(M.t/ms, M.v[0])
plt.xlabel('Time (ms)')
plt.ylabel('Membrane potential (v)')
plt.show()
```

Use Cases:

- Brain-machine interfaces
- Neuromorphic chips (Intel Loihi, IBM TrueNorth)
- Real-time signal processing

2. Neuroevolution

Neuroevolution is an approach where neural networks are evolved using genetic algorithms instead of being trained with backpropagation.

Key Features:

- Optimizes neural networks using evolutionary strategies.
- Useful in reinforcement learning and control problems.
- Works well in situations where gradient-based methods struggle.

Python Code: Evolving a Simple Neural Network

```
import numpy as np

# Define a simple neural network
def neural_network(weights, inputs):
    return np.tanh(np.dot(weights, inputs))

# Fitness function
def fitness(weights):
    inputs = np.array([0.5, -0.2])  # Example input
    output = neural_network(weights, inputs)
    return -abs(output - 1)  # Want output close to 1

# Genetic Algorithm
def evolve():
    population = [np.random.randn(2) for _ in range(10)]  # 10
individuals
    for gen in range(50):  # 50 generations
        scores = [fitness(w) for w in population]
        top_indices = np.argsort(scores)[-5:]  # Select top 5
        best = [population[i] for i in top_indices]
        new_population = best + [w + np.random.randn(2) * 0.1
for w in best]  # Mutate
        population = new_population
    return population[0]

best_weights = evolve()
print("Best weights:", best_weights)
```

Use Cases:

- Autonomous robotics
- Game AI (NEAT algorithm in OpenAI Gym)
- Optimizing hyperparameters in deep learning

3. Physics-Informed Neural Networks (PINNs)

Physics-Informed Neural Networks (PINNs) integrate physical laws (e.g., differential equations) into neural networks for solving scientific problems.

Key Features:

- Incorporates domain knowledge into training.
- Solves differential equations without numerical solvers.
- Used in engineering, physics, and climate modeling.

Python Code: Solving a Simple Differential Equation

```python
import torch
import torch.nn as nn

# Define a simple neural network for PINN
class PINN(nn.Module):
    def __init__(self):
        super(PINN, self).__init__()
        self.fc1 = nn.Linear(1, 20)
        self.fc2 = nn.Linear(20, 20)
        self.fc3 = nn.Linear(20, 1)

    def forward(self, x):
        x = torch.tanh(self.fc1(x))
        x = torch.tanh(self.fc2(x))
        return self.fc3(x)

# Loss function based on physics constraints
def physics_loss(model, x):
    x.requires_grad = True
    y = model(x)
    dydx = torch.autograd.grad(y, x, torch.ones_like(y), create_graph=True)[0]
    return torch.mean((dydx + x) ** 2)  # Example: dy/dx = -x

# Training the network
model = PINN()
optimizer = torch.optim.Adam(model.parameters(), lr=0.01)

x_train = torch.linspace(0, 2, 100).view(-1, 1)
for epoch in range(1000):
    optimizer.zero_grad()
    loss = physics_loss(model, x_train)
    loss.backward()
    optimizer.step()

print("Trained PINN Model Ready!")
```

Use Cases:

- Fluid dynamics (Navier-Stokes equations)
- Climate modeling
- Quantum mechanics

4. Capsule Networks

Capsule Networks (CapsNets) are an alternative to CNNs that model spatial relationships between features.

Key Features:

- Encodes hierarchical relationships.
- Handles affine transformations better than CNNs.
- Used for medical imaging and 3D object recognition.

Python Code: Capsule Network (Simplified)

```
import tensorflow as tf
from tensorflow.keras import layers, models

# Simple capsule layer
class CapsuleLayer(layers.Layer):
    def __init__(self, num_capsules, dim_capsules):
        super(CapsuleLayer, self).__init__()
        self.num_capsules = num_capsules
        self.dim_capsules = dim_capsules

    def call(self, inputs):
        return  tf.norm(inputs,  axis=-1,  keepdims=True)    #
Squash function

input_layer = layers.Input(shape=(28, 28, 1))
conv = layers.Conv2D(32, (9,9), activation='relu')(input_layer)
caps_layer = CapsuleLayer(10, 16)(conv)

model            =            models.Model(inputs=input_layer,
outputs=caps_layer)
model.summary()
```

Use Cases:

- Handwritten digit recognition

- Object recognition in cluttered images
- Medical imaging

5. Hypernetworks

Hypernetworks are networks that generate weights for another neural network, enabling dynamic adaptation.

Key Features:

- Produces weights on-the-fly instead of learning fixed weights.
- Reduces storage requirements.
- Used in meta-learning and few-shot learning.

Python Code: Simple Hypernetwork

```python
import torch

class Hypernetwork(nn.Module):
    def __init__(self):
        super(Hypernetwork, self).__init__()
        self.fc = nn.Linear(2, 4)  # Generates weights

    def forward(self, x):
        return self.fc(x)  # Generate weights dynamically

hypernet = Hypernetwork()
x = torch.randn(1, 2)
weights = hypernet(x)
print(weights)
```

Use Cases:

- Few-shot learning
- Neural architecture search
- Dynamic AI models

Conclusion

Neural networks go beyond deep learning and are applied to various fields such as neuroevolution, physics-informed modeling, and hypernetworks. These approaches provide alternative ways of using AI for tasks where traditional deep learning may not be the best fit.

Ethical Considerations in AI

Ethical Considerations in AI for Neural Networks
As neural networks become more powerful, their widespread use raises ethical concerns. These concerns range from **bias and fairness** to **privacy, security, accountability, and environmental impact**. Below are key ethical issues and how they affect AI development.

1. Bias and Fairness

Neural networks learn from data, which can contain human biases. If not carefully managed, AI can reinforce **racial, gender, or socioeconomic discrimination**.

Key Issues:

- **Bias in training data:** AI models inherit biases from historical data (e.g., biased hiring practices).
- **Unfair decision-making:** AI-driven systems in banking, healthcare, or criminal justice can disproportionately impact certain groups.
- **Lack of diversity in datasets:** Insufficient representation of minority groups leads to poor performance in real-world applications.

Example:

A hiring algorithm trained on historical data from a male-dominated industry might **unintentionally discriminate** against women.

Solution Approaches:
- Use **fairness-aware algorithms** (e.g., IBM AI Fairness 360).
- Audit and test models for biased outcomes before deployment.
- Improve dataset diversity and transparency.

2. Privacy and Data Security

Neural networks rely on vast amounts of **personal data**, raising privacy risks. AI models can also leak sensitive information through unintended behaviors.

Key Issues:

- **Data misuse:** Companies collect and store large datasets, which can be hacked or misused.
- **Inference attacks:** AI models can leak sensitive details, even when anonymized.
- **Surveillance concerns:** Facial recognition and tracking AI can be used for mass surveillance.

Example:

A facial recognition AI used for security can be misused by **authoritarian regimes** for **mass surveillance**, violating privacy rights.

Solution Approaches:

- Use **privacy-preserving AI techniques** like **differential privacy** and **federated learning**.
- Implement strict **data governance policies**.
- Develop AI that minimizes **data retention** and collection.

3. Explainability and Accountability

Many neural networks, especially deep learning models, act as **black boxes**—making decisions without clear explanations.

Key Issues:
- **Lack of transparency:** AI decisions in **healthcare, finance, and legal** fields must be explainable.
- **Who is responsible?** If an AI model makes an unfair or dangerous decision, **who is accountable**—the developer, company, or the AI itself?
- **Regulatory challenges:** Laws like the **EU AI Act** demand explainability in AI decision-making.

Example:

An AI-driven **loan approval system** denies applications without explaining why, making it difficult to appeal unfair decisions.

Solution Approaches:
- Use **Explainable AI (XAI)** techniques to improve model transparency.
- Enforce AI regulations that require human oversight in critical applications.
- Encourage AI audits and ethical reviews before deployment.

4. Environmental Impact

Training large neural networks consumes **massive amounts of energy**, contributing to **carbon emissions** and environmental damage.

Key Issues:

- **High energy consumption:** Training **GPT-4** required **megawatt-hours** of electricity.
- **E-waste from AI hardware:** GPUs and TPUs used in AI training have **high carbon footprints**.

- **Environmental inequality:** AI research is dominated by companies in developed nations, leaving underprivileged regions with **high energy costs**.

Example:

A study found that training a **single deep learning model** can emit as much **carbon dioxide** as five cars over their lifetime.

Solution Approaches:
- Optimize AI training efficiency (e.g., using **pruning, quantization, and knowledge distillation**).
- Use renewable energy for AI model training.
- Promote sustainable AI practices, such as **low-power AI models**.

5. Autonomous AI and Job Displacement

As AI systems automate tasks, they impact **jobs and the economy**, raising concerns about **unemployment and income inequality**.

Key Issues:

- **Automation replacing jobs:** AI can replace workers in industries like **manufacturing, customer service, and transportation**.
- **Economic disparity:** AI benefits **large corporations** more than small businesses, widening the economic gap.
- **Need for reskilling:** Workers must **adapt** to new AI-driven roles.

Example:

Self-driving AI in **trucking and delivery** could eliminate **millions of jobs** in transportation.

Solution Approaches:

- Governments should create **AI-driven reskilling programs**.
- Companies should integrate AI **alongside** human workers rather than replacing them.
- Implement **universal basic income (UBI)** experiments to mitigate economic disruption.

6. AI in Warfare and Autonomous Weapons

AI-powered weapons and **autonomous military drones** raise serious ethical concerns.

Key Issues:

- **Lethal Autonomous Weapons Systems (LAWS):** AI-controlled weapons can operate without human intervention.
- **Ethical dilemmas in combat:** AI decisions on **life and death** could be unethical.
- **Potential for misuse:** Terrorist organizations could exploit AI-based weapons.

Example:

Countries are developing AI-powered **combat drones** that can identify and eliminate targets without human control.

Solution Approaches:

- Enforce **global regulations on AI weapons** (e.g., UN discussions on banning autonomous weapons).
- Ensure **human oversight in AI-based warfare**.
- Develop AI systems aligned with **ethical military standards**.

Conclusion

Neural networks bring powerful innovations but also pose **ethical risks**. Developers, policymakers, and researchers must address these concerns through **bias mitigation, privacy safeguards, explainability, sustainability, and human oversight**.

Quantum Neural Networks (QNNs): A Look Ahead

Quantum Neural Networks (QNNs) combine **quantum computing** with **artificial neural networks** to achieve better efficiency and performance in certain computational tasks. While classical neural networks rely on standard matrix operations, QNNs leverage **quantum superposition, entanglement, and interference** to process information differently.

Key Features of QNNs:

☑ **Parallelism**: Quantum systems can process multiple states at once (superposition).
☑ **Exponential Speedup**: Certain problems (e.g., optimization, cryptography) may see **exponential acceleration** with quantum computing.
☑ **Quantum Gates**: Replaces classical activation functions with quantum unitary operations.
☑ **Hybrid Models**: Combines quantum and classical neural networks for practical applications.

1. Quantum Circuits for Neural Networks

A basic **Quantum Neural Network (QNN)** consists of:
- **Quantum neurons** (qubits instead of classical perceptrons).
- **Quantum gates** for transformations.
- **Measurement** to extract results from quantum states.

Example: Building a Simple QNN with PennyLane

PennyLane (by Xanadu) is a Python library for quantum machine learning.

Installing PennyLane

If you haven't installed it, run:

pip install pennylane

Code: Simple Quantum Neuron

This example simulates a **quantum perceptron** using a **qubit rotation** as an activation function.

```
import pennylane as qml
import numpy as np

# Define a quantum device with one qubit
dev = qml.device("default.qubit", wires=1)

@qml.qnode(dev)
def quantum_neuron(theta):
    """Quantum perceptron using a qubit rotation as
activation."""
    qml.RY(theta, wires=0)  # Rotate qubit state by theta
    qml.Hadamard(wires=0)  # Introduce superposition
    return qml.expval(qml.PauliZ(0))  # Measure qubit state

# Example: Applying a quantum rotation
theta = np.pi / 4  # Input value
output = quantum_neuron(theta)
print(f"Quantum Neuron Output: {output:.4f}")
```

Explanation:

1. **Qubit Rotation**: The input theta modifies the quantum state.
2. **Hadamard Gate**: Introduces superposition to increase expressiveness.
3. **Measurement**: Extracts results from the quantum state.

2. Hybrid Quantum-Classical Neural Network

Since full-scale QNNs require **quantum hardware**, many practical approaches use **hybrid models**, where **some layers are classical, and others are quantum**.

Code: Hybrid QNN with PennyLane and PyTorch

This example builds a **hybrid neural network** where:
- **Classical layers** process data.
- **Quantum layers** handle feature transformations.

```python
import torch
import torch.nn as nn
import pennylane as qml

# Quantum device with 2 qubits
n_qubits = 2
dev = qml.device("default.qubit", wires=n_qubits)

# Quantum Circuit Layer
def quantum_layer(inputs, weights):
    qml.AngleEmbedding(inputs, wires=range(n_qubits))
    qml.StronglyEntanglingLayers(weights,
wires=range(n_qubits))
    return qml.expval(qml.PauliZ(0))

# Convert to Torch Layer
class QuantumLayer(nn.Module):
    def __init__(self, n_qubits, n_layers):
        super().__init__()
        weight_shapes = {"weights": (n_layers, n_qubits, 3)}
        self.qnode = qml.qnode(dev)(quantum_layer)
        self.qlayer      =      qml.qnn.TorchLayer(self.qnode,
weight_shapes)

    def forward(self, x):
        return self.qlayer(x)

# Hybrid Neural Network
class HybridQNN(nn.Module):
    def __init__(self):
        super().__init__()
        self.fc1 = nn.Linear(4, 2) # Classical layer
```

```
    self.q_layer = QuantumLayer(n_qubits=2, n_layers=2) #
Quantum layer
    self.fc2 = nn.Linear(1, 1)  # Output layer

  def forward(self, x):
    x = torch.tanh(self.fc1(x))
    x = self.q_layer(x)
    x = torch.sigmoid(self.fc2(x))
    return x

# Initialize model
model = HybridQNN()
inputs      =      torch.tensor([[0.5,      -0.1,      0.3,      0.7]],
dtype=torch.float32)
output = model(inputs)
print("Hybrid QNN Output:", output.item())
```

Explanation:

1. **Classical Layer (fc1)**: Transforms the input using a dense layer.
2. **Quantum Layer (q_layer)**: Processes transformed inputs via a **quantum circuit** (implemented using StronglyEntanglingLayers).
3. **Final Layer (fc2)**: Outputs a **classical prediction**.

3. Future Applications of QNNs

Quantum neural networks are still in early research stages but show promise in:

Application	How QNNs Help
Optimization Problems	Faster solutions to **logistics, finance, and scheduling** tasks.
Drug Discovery	Simulating molecular interactions using quantum states.
Quantum Cryptography	Secure encryption and key distribution.
Financial Modeling	Simulating market trends with **quantum Monte Carlo methods**.
AI in Quantum Chemistry	Designing materials using quantum simulations.

4. Challenges and Limitations

Challenge	Current Limitation
Quantum Hardware	Real quantum computers have **high noise and low qubit counts**.
Scalability	QNNs struggle with **scaling beyond a few qubits** due to decoherence.
Hybrid Integration	Bridging quantum and classical layers remains an **open research** problem.
Lack of Software Tools	Quantum ML tools (e.g., PennyLane, Qiskit) are still **early-stage**.

Future Outlook

- **Near-term**: **Hybrid QNNs** will be useful before full quantum models become viable.
- **Long-term**: More stable **quantum processors** (e.g., **Google's Sycamore, IBM Quantum**) will unlock larger-scale QNNs.

Conclusion

Quantum Neural Networks (QNNs) offer exciting possibilities but require **better quantum hardware** for practical use. Hybrid models that mix **classical and quantum computing** provide a more feasible approach today.

www.ingramcontent.com/pod-product-compliance
Lightning Source LLC
La Vergne TN
LVHW051338050326
832903LV00031B/3609